967.571 Destexhe, Alain.
D
         Rwanda and genocide
         in the twentieth
         century.

$19.95

BAKER & TAYLOR

Rwanda and Genocide in the Twentieth Century

Rwanda and Genocide in the Twentieth Century

ALAIN DESTEXHE

Translated by Alison Marschner

Foreword by William Shawcross

NEW YORK UNIVERSITY PRESS
Washington Square, New York

First published in the U.S.A. in 1995 by
NEW YORK UNIVERSITY PRESS
Washington Square
New York, N.Y.   10003

Library of Congress Cataloging-in-Publication Data
Destexhe, Alain.
     [Rwanda, essai sur le genocide. English]
     Rwanda and genocide in the twentieth century / Alain Destexhe;
translated by Alison Marschner.
          p.   cm.
     Includes bibliographical references.
     ISBN 0–8147–1873–6
     1. Rwanda—History—Civil War, 1994. 2. Genocide—Rwanda.
I. Title.
DT450.435.R8513   1995
967.57104—dc20   95–17419
                                                                              CIP

Printed in Great Britain

Contents

Translator's Note

Anyone turning from the original French version of this book to this English edition will quickly realise that this is very far from being a straightforward translation. Alain Destexhe was writing to a deadline while events were still evolving but the preparation of the English text has not been subject to such restrictions. I have therefore been able to incorporate updates and revisions, in agreement with the author, particularly where these seemed appropriate to an English-speaking readership.

Alison Marschner

Foreword

In the last 50 years one can say that there have been three different periods of strife, three different kinds of warfare.

In the first, during and just after the Second World War, conflict was classical – states fighting each other.

In the second period, decolonisation and the Cold War, governments fought guerrilla liberation movements, which were often based on desire for independence and on some form of political morality. The Cold War established certain patterns. In most conflicts there was polarisation induced by the bipolar world. There was a framework in which the parties were identified.

Since the fall of the Berlin Wall, established patterns are gone. Now there is often a surplus of parties or interlocutors. We are now in a period of non-structured or destructured conflict – as in Somalia, Liberia, Rwanda, Bosnia – which is sometimes called 'identity based'. Now there is something approaching chaos in international relations. At least disorder.

Alain Destexhe has been closely involved in these changes, as the Secretary General of Médecins Sans Frontières. He has struggled with the complexities and contradictions on the ground. And, what makes his work particularly valuable, he has attempted to put them into a political, legal and philosophical context.

This book is very important. It is both lucid, calmly argued, and passionate. It confronts some of the most urgent issues of the post-Cold War world and attempts to deal with the new World Disorder that has followed the fall of the Wall. In particular it looks at genocide.

He points out that although D-Day, VE Day and *Schindler's List* have been celebrated, their lessons have not been applied to the present. 'Never Again!' has been exposed as a slogan not a promise. His book, he writes, is 'an indictment against the apparent inability to relate the present to the past which may result in a future amnesty for those responsible for genocide'.

Destexhe rightly takes Nuremberg as his starting point or bench mark. He dismisses the ghastly attempts at moral equivalence by those, for example, who attempt to equate Hiroshima with the Holocaust. He rejects the term genocide in connection with the Nigerian war against Biafra, and in Vietnam. In Bosnia, he argues, the Serbs have been the most guilty party, carrying out crimes against humanity but not genocide as such. Their objective was territory, not people. In the end, he defines only three fully fledged cases of genocide during the twentieth century – the Armenians by the Turks, the Jews by the Nazis and that of the Tutsis by the Hutus in Rwanda only last year.

It is useless to blame today's tragedies on the mistakes of decades ago. But one characteristic of genocide on which he insists is that it results from orders given by those in authority. Destexhe describes how the Belgian colonisers exploited the differences between the Hutus and Tutsis for their own administrative purposes, making the minority Tutsis the rulers over the Hutu majority.

But when western concepts of what was right began to change in the late 1950s, so the Belgians began to feel more sympathy for the Hutus and to promote their cause – and thus exacerbate tensions. In the end it was the ethnic classification system of identity cards introduced by the Belgians that enabled the Hutu regime to carry out the genocide of Tutsis last year.

He identifies radio broadcasts as one of the most powerful factors in the genocidal campaign by the Hutu. In much of Africa, and other parts of the developing world, a transistor radio is the only source of information. In Rwanda, Radio Mille Collines, set up by associates of the Hutu president in 1993, began broadcasting terrible messages of hate such as 'the grave is only half full. Who will help us fill it?' After the genocide began in April 1994, Radio Milles Collines announced, 'By 5 May, the country must be completely cleansed of Tutsis.' It helped convince Hutu peasants that they were under threat and urged them to 'make the Tutsis smaller' by decapitating them.

How did the world react? Barely at all. The Security Council left the Tutsi to their fate. Why? Because the United States was 'haunted by the ghost of Somalia', where thirty of its soldiers had died. When the massacres began, almost all foreigners were evacuated. General Romeo Dallaire, the commander of the UN forces in Kigali, asked for reinforcements and later said that with 5000 troops he could have saved 500,000 people. Instead the contingent was cut to 270. The world ran away.

The Security Council refused to accept the massacres were genocide, for that would have compelled them to intervene under international law. The UN was prepared to act only 'under the ambiguous banner of humanitarianism'. Yet, as Médecins Sans Frontières has said, 'Genocide Cannot be Stopped by Doctors'. Operation Turquoise, the short French government deployment, undoubtedly saved lives, but it did nothing to resolve the chaos, still less to bring anyone to justice.

It was not until the mass exodus of refugees first to Tanzania and then to Goma in Zaire that CNN and other international television stations began really to pay attention to Rwanda. The world responded well to the refugee crisis, with an outpouring of aid. The problem was that the camps were often controlled by the very people who had ordered the killings of the Tutsis – men who should have been put on trial rather than assisted by the international community. As a result of humanitarianism, the killers have had their strength and their authority restored. And why? Because, as so often today, humanitarianism is a figleaf for political inaction.

Today, where humanitarianism seems the only possible form of international action, 'all catastrophes are treated alike and reduced to their lowest common denominator – compassion on the part of the onlooker'.

In Bosnia and elsewhere, humanitarianism has been used to mask the failure of political will. It has been more than a mask; it has become a diversion. This is not to say that humanitarianism is useless or not needed – but that it is increasingly abused.

Destexhe urges that the perpetrators of the Rwandan genocide be put on trial. For the sake of the actual victims, to protect other groups from similar attacks, and for the sake of humanity itself. At Nuremberg – one of the most important legal landmarks of the twentieth century – the real plaintiff was Civilisation itself; so it should be again today.

The crime of genocide affects the whole human race, but the Genocide Convention has never reached its obvious conclusion – the creation of an international court to judge the facts and to sentence the guilty.

Destexhe argues that Nuremberg merely advanced Montesquieu's idea that international law is 'universal civil law, in the sense that all peoples are citizens of the universe'.

Put in a different way, Nuremberg was, in the words of Rebecca West, a legalistic prayer that the kingdom of heaven be with us. It is not yet. Rwanda and Bosnia both show that the need for a Tribunal is more urgent than ever. Exactly 50 years after Nuremberg its precedents must be established in international law and put into effect.

Alain Destexhe's study is essential to an understanding of the need.

William Shawcross

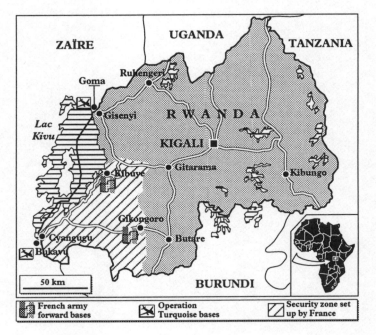

Source: *Libération*

CHAPTER 1

The Unlearned Lesson of History

The discovery of the Nazi concentration camps at the end of the Second World War may have aroused shock and horror throughout the world and raised the popular cry, 'Never again!' but other voices were less certain that this particular lesson of history had really been learned. The Italian writer, Primo Levi, who himself survived Auschwitz, rejected the idea that the camps could be explained away either as an accident of history or an expression of mid-twentieth century barbarism. He saw the risk that they could well serve as an exemplary model for today's world: 'The simple fact is that it has happened once, and it could all happen again.'[1]

In 1994, the 50th anniversary of D-Day was widely commemorated, with great ceremony and much media coverage. The same year also saw the release of Steven Spielberg's film *Schindler's List*, widely acclaimed by millions of cinemagoers. Such events revived the memories of those who lived through the war years and kindled interest among younger generations. It is clear that they stimulated so much discussion about the genocide of the Jews that there can be no doubt that the victims will be remembered well beyond the lifetimes of the remaining survivors.

It is, however, questionable whether this revival of interest in the Second World War and the genocide of the Jews is really contributing towards a better understanding of contemporary situations comparable with some aspects of these events. How many of those who wept during Spielberg's film shed tears for the victims of the recent massacres in Bosnia or in Rwanda? Yet of what use is the past if we do not learn from it ways of helping us deal with the present? Surely the main lesson to be learned from the extermination of the Jews

1

is that we must prevent further genocides. What is the point of remembering this largest of genocides if we at the same time do nothing to prevent the massacre of half a million Tutsis over a few weeks in Rwanda? We claim to be rebuilding Europe on the idealism of 'Never again!' and yet allow ethnic cleansing to continue in the very heart of the continent.

It must of course be made quite clear that using Auschwitz as a measuring stick when making comparisons with other situations risks trivialising and minimising the real nature of the genocide perpetrated against the Jews and seeing it as the inevitable consequence of political and social evils that prevailed at the time. This is not the intention. Yet the extermination of the Jews is in fact the only precedent which *can* be evoked to understand the crime committed against the Tutsis in Rwanda, for both Jews and Tutsis were targeted as victims because, and only because, they had the misfortune to be born Jews or Tutsis. Those who killed them committed the very worst of crimes, described by François de Menthon, the French prosecutor at the Nuremberg Trials, as 'the crime which is directed at the very nature of what it is to be human'. Just as wearing the yellow star singled out the Jews living under Nazi rule, so too the ethnic classification on Tutsi identity cards acted as a death warrant allowing the first genocide since the end of the Second World War.

These are the thoughts out of which this book has grown: an indictment against the apparent inability to relate the present to the past; a failing which could result in an amnesty for those responsible for genocide.

The Crime of Genocide

Genocide is distinguishable from all other crimes by the motivation behind it. Towards the end of the Second World War, when the full horror of the extermination and concentration camps became public knowledge, Winston Churchill stated that the world was being brought face to face with 'a crime that has no name'. History was of little use in finding a recognised word to fit the nature of the crime that Nazi Germany, a modern, industrialised state, had engaged in. There simply were no precedents in regard to either the nature or the degree of the crime. Raphaël Lemkin, the Polish-born adviser to the United States War Ministry, saw that the world was being confronted with a totally unprecedented phenomena and that 'new conceptions require new terminology'. In his book, *Axis Rule in Occupied Europe*, published in 1944, he coined the word 'genocide', constructed, in contradiction to the accepted rules of etymology, from the Greek 'genos' (race or tribe) and the Latin suffix 'cide' (to kill). According to Lemkin, genocide signifies 'the destruction of a nation or of an ethnic group'[2] and implies the existence of a coordinated plan, aimed at total extermination, to be put into effect against individuals chosen as victims purely, simply and exclusively because they are members of the target group.

Criminal Intention

According to Raphaël Lemkin, the expression 'mass murder' that was being used at the time to describe what had happened was an inadequate description of the totally new phenomenon witnessed in Nazi-occupied territories. It was inadequate because it failed to account for the motive for the crime, which arose solely from 'racial, national or religious' considerations and had nothing to do with the conduct of the war. War crimes had been defined for the first time in 1907 in The Hague Convention, but the crime of genocide required a separate definition as this was 'not only a crime against the rules of war, but a crime against humanity itself' affecting not just the individual or nation in question, but humanity as a whole. Raphaël Lemkin was the first person to put forward the theory that genocide is not a war crime and that the immorality of a crime such as genocide should not be confused with the amorality of war.[3]

The definition of what constitutes a crime against humanity was established at the Nuremberg Trials. However, despite the significance of this, the jurists at Nuremberg had invented nothing new. They were simply advancing Montesquieu's ideas on international law, which he described as 'universal civil law, in the sense that all peoples are citizens of the universe'.[4] Killing someone simply because he or she exists is a crime against humanity;[5] it is a crime against the very essence of what it is to be human. This is not an elimination of individuals because they are political adversaries, or because they hold to what are regarded as false beliefs or dangerous theories, but a crime directed against the person as a person, against the very humanity of the individual victim. Thus it cannot be categorised as a war crime. As Alain Finkielkraut, the French philosopher, has pointed out, it is quite a different thing to be regarded as an enemy than as a particular species of vermin to be systematically wiped out.[6]

Genocide is a crime on a different scale to all other crimes against humanity and implies an intention to completely exterminate the chosen group. Genocide is therefore both the gravest and the greatest of the crimes against humanity:

> In the same way as in a case of homicide the natural right of the individual to exist is implied, so in the case of genocide as a crime, the principle that any national, racial or religious group has a natural right to exist is clearly evident. Attempts to eliminate such groups violate this right to exist and to develop within the international community.[7]

A genocide is a conspiracy aimed at the total destruction of a group and thus requires a concerted plan of action. The instigators and initiators of a genocide are cool-minded theorists first and barbarians only second. The specificity of genocide does not arise from the extent of the killings, nor their savagery or resulting infamy, but solely from the intention: the destruction of a group.

Lemkin's efforts and his single-minded perseverance brought about the Convention for the Prevention and the Punishment of the Crime of Genocide which was voted into existence by the General Assembly of the United Nations (UN) in 1948. After stating in Article 1 that genocide is a crime under international law, the Convention laid down the following definition:

any of the following acts committed with intent to destroy, in whole or in part, a national, ethnical, racial or religious group, as such:

a killing members of the group;
b causing serious bodily or mental harm to members of the group;
c deliberately inflicting on the group conditions of life calculated to bring about its physical destruction in whole or in part;
d imposing measures intended to prevent births within the group;
e forcibly transferring children of the group to another group.*

This definition, although lessening the uniqueness of Lemkin's concept to some extent, is nonetheless of remarkable significance. Some UN member states wanted to go further to include the notion of cultural or economic genocide, others would have added political motivations. The French representative remarked at the time, 'even if crimes of genocide were committed for racial or religious reasons in the past, it is clear that the motivation for such crimes in future will be mainly political'.[8] Ironically, and probably not without ulterior motives, the Soviet delegate gave the real reason for the exclusion of politically-defined groups arguing that their inclusion would be contrary to the 'scientific' definition of genocide and would reduce the effectiveness of the Convention if it could then be applied to any political crime whatsoever.

The final definition as it stands today is based on four constituent factors:

• a criminal act, ...
• with the intention of destroying ...
• an ethnic, national or religious group, ...
• targeted as such.

If it was the reality of the Genocide that led to the establishment of the concept of genocide, in most people's minds there was an almost automatic connection between the two.

* See Appendix 1

Consequently the word 'genocide' has often been used when making comparisons with later massacres throughout the world in order to attract attention by evoking images of the concentration camps and their victims. The Second World War and the genocide became absolute references in the political context. As Alain Finkielkraut puts it, 'Satan became incarnate in the person of Hitler who represented nothing less than an allegory for the devil.'[9] Fascism became the supreme enemy and all political adversaries were indiscriminately accused of supporting it. But it was genocide that became the ultimate verbal stigma, a term used both to describe any thoroughly horrendous, thoroughly fascist act perpetrated by an enemy and as a rallying call for minority groups looking to assert their identity and legitimise their existence. Thus the word genocide fell victim to a sort of verbal inflation, in much the same as happened with the word fascist. It has been applied freely and indiscriminately to groups as diverse as the blacks of South Africa, Palestinians and women, as well as in reference to animals, abortion, famines and widespread malnutrition, and to many other situations.

The term genocide has progressively lost its initial meaning and is becoming dangerously commonplace. In order to shock people and gain their attention to contemporary situations of violence or injustice by making comparisons with murder on the greatest scale known in this century, 'genocide' has been used as synonymous with massacre, oppression and repression, overlooking that what lies behind the image it evokes is the attempted annihilation of the entire Jewish race. One of the aims of this book is to restore the specific meaning to a term which has been so much abused that it has become the victim of its own success. Further trivialisation has resulted from the over-use of the term 'Holocaust', first popularised on a wide scale in the 1970s by the American television series with that title. The original context is of course religious and means, literally, 'a ritual sacrifice wholly consumed by fire'. The use of this term has a twofold effect, both mystifying and spectacular, which distorts and denies reality.

The inevitable consequences of such misuse of language are a loss of meaning and a distortion of values. For example, there is a great danger in the way the media applied the term

'Holocaust' to the devastation wrought by the cholera epidemic in Goma, which has the largest concentration of Rwandan refugees in Zaire. This puts the medical disaster that resulted from the massive influx of refugees as a consequence of the genocide on the same level as the genocide itself, a premeditated mass-crime, systematically planned and executed. This has resulted in a double error with the exaggerated emphasis focused on the cholera victims – catastrophe though that was – distracting attention from the real crime already committed. The fact that cholera does not handpick its victims according to their ethnic origin was completely overlooked. (Even the controversial carpet-bombings that took place over Germany and Vietnam claimed their victims in a totally haphazard manner.) Intrinsic meaning is lost when a word is used so loosely to describe any human disaster with a large number of victims, regardless of the cause. As a further consequence, we arrive at a situation where no individuals are to be singled out as guilty or responsible because blame is laid at the door of historical fate and 'unfortunate circumstances', 'the climate of the time' and sheer bad luck. It would be hard to deny that some form of evil has always existed in the world. But if such evil is seen in general, impersonal terms such as barbarism, 'man's inhumanity to man', chance circumstance or plain hatred, then there are no individual culprits at whom an accusing finger can be pointed. On the other hand, if everyone is considered to be somehow involved and therefore somehow responsible, then the picture becomes hazy and guilt and innocence are somehow confused. This so-called collective blame is just another way of denying the facts.

The Importance of Making Distinctions

Many people would claim that the origin of a tragedy, be it natural causes or manmade, is of little importance compared with the suffering of the victims and those close to them. It is certainly true that all victims, without distinction, merit compassion and assistance. They all have the right to justice and to know that their suffering will not be forgotten. But

there are several reasons why it nonetheless remains essential
to distinguish between different sorts of tragedy.

First of all, such distinctions correspond to the different
kinds of reasoning and motivation that lie behind different
crimes. The elimination of political opponents, real or
assumed, is quite clearly a different crime from the planned
extermination of individuals on the basis of their racial or
ethnic group. It is not simply a question of establishing a scale
of values in regard to such terrible crimes, but of understanding the political mechanisms which are at work in each
instance. The large-scale massacres of the twentieth century
are the result of the most widespread totalitarian ideologies:
fascism, Stalinism, Maoism. The atrocities, the cold-blooded
murders, the planned elimination of hundreds of thousands
of people by Stalin and others in the name of a new enlightenment, resulted in a total number of victims that greatly
exceeded the number of Jews who perished in the genocide.
From Stalin to Mao, from Pol Pot's Cambodia to Mengistu's
Ethiopia, from the Vietnamese boat people to the Afghan
refugees, the victims must be counted in tens of millions.
In the 1930s, as Robert Conquest says in his important
historical work, *The Harvest of Sorrow*, Stalin's policy to
repress the *kulaks* in the Ukraine resulted in at least six
million victims.[10] In revolutionary China, the Great Leap
Forward, the product of one man's wild imagination, led to
a famine that produced a horrendous death toll of anything
from 16 to 42 million people. The Cultural Revolution, the
inspiration of the same man's desperate attempt to retain
the power that seemed to be slipping from him, caused a
further million deaths. In the face of such statistics, it is
surprising that the infamy of these crimes of communism,
in particular those of Stalin and Mao, have not yet been fully
recognised.

The greatest danger today arises from the re-birth of racist
ideologies that consider it 'logical' to classify different races
and ethnic groups, excluding and rejecting 'the other', even
when such classification leads to policies that advocate
wholesale slaughter on the basis of birth, religion or culture.
Such ideologies are to be found almost everywhere. In Africa,
policies of ethnic exclusiveness are practised in Zaire, in Sudan

and in Liberia, to cite only a few countries. In the Caucusus, population exchanges have become a commonplace way of settling conflicts, while in Burma, the concept of 'Burmese purity' affirms the supremacy of one group over all others – and in the heart of Europe itself, both of these ideas seem well set for a promising future. Islamic fundamentalism exudes a violence of another kind. Almost everywhere in the world we see recurring hatred of 'the other', leading to ethnic cleansing and racism: it is the greatest danger that we face today. And it is precisely this selective killing of 'the other', who is identified, targeted and slaughtered as such, that is at the root of a genocide.

Another reason why it is of fundamental importance to make distinctions between different kinds of catastrophes is that they are then revealed to vary greatly both in nature and in degree. However, the increasing amount of exaggerated news coverage given to any disaster, natural or manmade, nearly always infers that these events have one common denominator: they are seen as the product of fate and misfortune rather than the deliberate policy of any one individual or group. This results from the inability of the general public to make clear distinctions (value judgements) between a genocide and a civil war, a mugging and a road accident, famine, cholera epidemics and natural disasters. Massacres and killings are put down to barbarism, age-old hatreds, ancient fears and tribal wars: ambiguous terms rooted in the racial thinking of the nineteenth century which often sowed the seeds of much later hostility. For example, the first real signs of antagonism between the Serbs and Croats only surfaced at the beginning of the twentieth century; and it was after 1960, in the countrysides of Burundi and Rwanda, where the populations mainly lived, that the social differences between Hutu and Tutsi ceased to be seen as such and became an ethnic divide.

This simplification of issues can be seen everywhere, not only within the media but also in supposedly learned works on the subject, such as a recent collection with the already ambiguous title *L'histoire inhumaine: massacres et génocides des origines à nos jours*. From the first page onwards, we are told that at the root of all massacres 'there is always fear, from whence comes hatred', and the author concludes:

> The world seemed to have known the heights of horror with Nazism, the extermination camps and the holocaust of the Jews (the Shoah), but on 6 August 1945, the United States, the world's leading democratic country ... dropped the first atomic bomb in history on Hiroshima. ... Thus did terror make its entry into history on a global scale.[11]

The author, Guy Richard, not only trivialises the genocide committed by the Nazis, but, no doubt involuntarily, he implies that the two atrocities can be measured within the same set of values, oblivious to the totally different motivations that lay behind each of them. By giving equal significance to both events he even infers that the United States could be held responsible (guilty perhaps?) for a new and worse form of barbarism. In the face of this slanted argument, one almost hesitates to point out that it was Japan and Germany that declared war on the rest of the world and not the other way around, and that the aims of the Nazis and their system of values were far from the same as those of the Allies. The destruction of Dresden, unnecessary and criminal as it was, must also be understood as the response – albeit exaggerated, horrendous and futile – to Coventry, Rotterdam and Warsaw. But the bombs that fell on Dresden and the shells fired by both sides in the First World War (and if any war can be termed a butchery it is this) did not pre-select a race or a people as their victims. The pilot who dropped the bomb on Hiroshima was involved in fighting a war, not trying to exterminate the Japanese and deny their right to live as any other people. Although the government was prepared to commit a crime in order to hasten the end of the war, it did not do so by selecting the Japanese or the Germans as enemies and categorising them as a sub-human species. It should be clear that fear was not the source of the Second World War but rather, as with all widespread massacres, the source lay in individuals and their ideologies. It cannot be denied, therefore, that ultimately it must always be possible to pinpoint certain individuals responsible for carrying the guilt of their actions and making them face the consequences.

It is totally unacceptable and even dangerous to group together all those who die in tragic circumstances, regardless of the way in which they die. It should be obvious that it is not at all the same thing to die from cholera in a refugee camp or as the targetted victim of ethnic cleansing in one's own home. If it were all one and the same, then there would be no more at stake than the right of all victims to our compassion. Crime and guilt then cease to be significant and the particularly horrible murder of one individual would be measured with the same stick as a mass killing.

Three million Polish Jews and three million Polish Catholics died between 1939 and 1945, but can the two be compared? With the exception of a tiny minority, all the Polish Jews died because they were the target of a campaign of persecution and systematic extermination. The mainly Catholic population was not singled out in this way for complete elimination, at least not at the beginning. They were the victims of the Soviet and German occupations of their country: the Soviets decimated the Polish élite and the Germans carried out large-scale killings, summary executions and ferocious 'reprisals'. The Poles were forced into slave labour and left to die in the concentration camps. However, even though there were a large number of Catholics in Auschwitz, 90 per cent of those who perished there were Jews. More than a million Jews died in the gas chambers and 75,000 Catholic political prisoners died of the privations of camp life and forced labour. We remember Auschwitz because there were survivors: there were almost no survivors in the five other extermination camps of the Final Solution: Lublin, Treblinka, Belzec, Sobibor and Kulmhof, which is probably why so few people can recognise all the names. But it must be stressed that if there is a difference in the nature and degree of every massacre, at the level of each person who participates in such a crime, every individual who killed Polish Catholics was just as guilty as others who killed Jews – and each member of the Rwandan Patriotic Front (RPF) who has committed atrocities is just as guilty as the individual members of the Rwandan Armed Forces who carried out the genocide – or as guilty as any murderer.

In the penal code, a clear distinction is made between non-assistance to persons in danger, complicity in a crime, premeditation and extenuating circumstances; and, in terms of sentence, the murder of a child is in a different category to that of an adult. Unfortunately, such distinctions are not made in the international arena where all crimes tend to be put under the same heading of barbarism. But crimes against humanity and large-scale massacres in this century have rarely been perpetrated by barbarians. The Nazis and the radical Hutus were not barbarians but rather clear-thinking, determined criminals. To call them barbarians is, to an extent, to dehumanise them, almost to absolve them from responsibilty.

Without such distinctions, the question of guilt is hidden behind a protective mask of 'extenuating circumstances' that removes responsibility for all such crimes. This is the subject of a recent study by Georges de Maleville of the 'so-called genocide of Armenians' in 1915: 'The Armenians were victims of a series of dreadful coincidences, the sum total of which determined the (subsequent) tragedy.'[12] This convoluted reasoning totally ignores the question of responsibility. History apparently has no more to examine than a list of coincidental circumstances which de Maleville itemises as follows:

1. The Armenians *themselves provoked the revenge* [my emphasis] taken by certain elements of the Ottoman population.
2. While there is no reason to hold the Union Party (the government party) partly responsible for this crime, nevertheless, once Enver and Talaat, the UP leaders, had taken the decision to proceed, it was put into effect with a quite *astounding lack of forethought* [my emphasis].
3. *To this lack of forethought, of which they were certainly guilty* [my emphasis], the Ottoman authorities could add a third factor: the disintegration of their empire.[13]

With this twisting of the facts, it is made to look as though the Armenians in some way committed suicide and the Young Turks were only guilty of a lack of forethought! Such reasoning shocks us when it is used by revisionist historians of the genocide of the Jews, but we do not sufficiently recognise how it is in regular use today to describe contemporary conflicts, such as in Bosnia and in Rwanda. In Rwanda, some commentators were very quick to explain that the killings were due to background 'circumstances': the war, the death of the Hutu president, the 'excesses of crowds gripped by fear and ancient hatred', the 'justifiable anger of the people', the 'provocations by the Tutsis' and their 'historical domination' of the country, etc.

A consequence of this kind of reasoning is that 'collective guilt' leaves us with no one to blame: no one admits to having chosen to become a Young Turk, a Nazi or a supporter of Stalin. Therefore, so the argument continues, genocides and systematic massacres fall into the same category of disaster as volcanic eruptions or earthquakes. Carl Jung is quoted as saying, 'The devil has always been around. He was there before the advent of human beings and he is the eternal principle that has corrupted them! So there will always be evil people. ... Thus blaming the devil ... is a providential convenience.'[14] Where then lies guilt and responsibility if blame is laid on the devil, on 'man's inhumanity to man', on circumstances or on destiny? – certainly it cannot then lie with any individual human beings.

Crimes differ as much in regard to their nature as to their degree and no two crimes can be measured with the same stick. To put it bluntly, even if Pinochet deserves the maximum penalty, the magnitude of his crime cannot be compared to the evil wrought by Stalin or Hitler. When a massacre occurs, no matter the circumstances, there will always be individuals who are responsible, and therefore guilty, and they must be designated as such. A clear distinction must be made between the executioner and his victims, although the argument that both sides may have committed atrocities is often raised in order to avoid addressing the issue. But such cruelties are not always comparable and only a cynic will rank together the Bosnian Serbs and the Bosnian government, or the previous Rwandan government and the present government. Their crimes are not comparable, neither in regard to intention, nor to nature nor to degree.

Finally, there is the larger question of international responsibility which varies according to the crime committed. When all such crimes are collated under one heading, the obligation on the part of the international community to intervene is more easily overlooked. Certainly, the international community cannot be expected to resolve every conflict and, until the end of the Cold War, international intervention to end the large-scale killings was not easy with two superpowers ruling the world. But the international context has now changed and the principal obstacles to intervention lie more in western public opinion than in any physical constraints on the ground. In the case of genocide, there is an international convention which binds the signatories to recognise that this is a crime against the whole of humanity. This recognition stems from the work of Raphaël Lemkin, who insisted that:

> to treat genocide as a crime that only concerns an individual nation makes no sense because by its very nature the author is either the state itself or powerful groups backed by the state. ... By its legal, moral and human nature, genocide must be regarded as an international crime.[15]

The crime of genocide *ipso facto* affects the entire human race but the Convention has never resulted in what should be its logical conclusion: the constitution of a permanent international court authorised to judge those accused of responsibility. Instead, each state jealously guards its sovereignty over its own legal territory with the result that, because they act as their own judges, the authors and instigators of such crime have the best possible guarantee of impunity. A genocide cannot be carried out without the participation or the complicity of the highest authorities in the state. Nevertheless, despite reservations about using it, the international community has the Convention at its disposal: a legal instrument that has been ratified by 120 countries and which, according to the International Court of Justice, holds to generally accepted values which oblige all states, even those which have few links with the international community, to 'punish and prevent genocide'.

Imperfect as the Convention may be, international responsibility is implied here to a far greater extent than with other crimes for which there are no similar conventions or for which the conventions hold no kind of international sanction. The Convention on Genocide clearly states that the authors and instigators of a genocide must be brought to trial and, under the conditions of Article 8, any government may call upon the competent UN bodies 'to take such action ... as they judge appropriate'. So far, however, no signatory government has judged it desirable to take advantage of these provisions. Yet there is nothing to prevent a state which is party to the Convention, even if it is not directly affected itself, from calling for sanctions against violations committed in another signatory country, as should be the case with Rwanda.[16]

Ultimately, the use of the term genocide must be severely limited to situations where it is actually applicable on all counts. Current misuse of the word and the convoluted reasoning that accompanies it must be resisted. If not, the real meaning of genocide will continue to be trivialised and this most anti-human of all crimes will continue to be regarded as one more reason to justify fatalism. Genocide must be reinstated as the most infamous of crimes, the memory of the victims preserved and those responsible identified and brought to justice by the international community.

Major Tragedies Since 1945

For reasons already put forward, despite the degree of horror of the crimes committed by Stalin, Mao and those who emulated them, we must refuse to qualify them as genocides. We must find other words to describe such post-Second World War tragedies and crises which have so often been referred to as genocides: the partition of India in 1947; Indonesia (1965–66); Biafra (1968–71); Bangladesh (1970–71); the Vietnam War (1965–73); Cambodia

(1975–79); Ethiopia (1984–85); Somalia (1991–92); Tibet (1951); the decimation of Indian tribes in the Amazon; and Bosnia (from 1992).

Genocide has often been the term used to describe famine situations. Yet 'famine' is itself a term that has been much abused. Famine is often confused with drought which, fortunately, only rarely entails catastrophe on a scale that might justify the description. In fact, with the exception of China's Greap Leap Forward, the world has only known three or four major famines since the 1940s: Biafra, Ethiopia and Somalia. The famine in South Sudan in 1988 which claimed at least 250,000 victims could justifiably be fourth on the list. All of these disasters were due to a combination of war and deliberate policy rather than to drought[17] and certainly none of them can be qualified as genocide, though it is difficult to pinpoint specific causes. In Somalia, the infamous 'warlords' are certainly largely responsible for the catastrophe that occured in the country at the beginning of this decade, but the roots of the problem lay deep within Somali society itself which, it could be said, was to blame for its own disintegration with the imposition of an imported one-party, authoritarian-style government onto a nomadic clan structure.[18] In Ethiopia, Mengistu's Marxist government must be held to blame, but its policy was aimed at building a new society rather than ethnic considerations.[19] The famine in Biafra, which historian John de Saint Jorre estimated, resulted in 600,000 deaths,[20] was the first tragedy to be played out on our television screens. It was the result of a deliberate blockade imposed by Nigerian government forces on the Biafran enclave and, to a lesser extent, deliberate manipulation of the food shortages by the Biafran secessionist government in order to influence world opinion. This conflict had an important ethnic dimension as Biafra was populated mainly by the Ibos. However, no matter what was being said at the time, government policy in Lagos was never dicated by ethnic considerations as can be confirmed by the measures taken to reintegrate the Ibos into the Nigerian community after the fall of Biafra.

The term genocide has been used on many occasions during the course of a conflict, in particular in regard to

Vietnam where it was used both by the French philosopher, Jean-Paul Sartre and by the Russell Tribunal. But American intentions were never to target the Vietnamese people specifically. America's objective was to win a major battle in the course of a Cold War between the two major powers that was fought entirely in countries other than their own. There was no questioning of the morality of the large-scale bombing inflicted on Vietnam as whole, whilst sparing Hanoi and other major cities. However, the facts did not prevent the war from being described as a genocide by those seeking to compare American bombing raids with the worst Nazi crimes.

Religious and ethnic confrontations have also been described as genocide. Such was the case in regard to the massacres of Hindus by Moslems and Moslems by Hindus during the partition of India in 1947. But despite the very large number of victims on both sides, they would be more appropriately qualified as large-scale pogroms and there is a fundamental difference between a pogrom and a process of genocidal extermination. A pogrom bears on both people and their belongings and is not intended to annihilate a whole people, contrary to a genocidal extermination process.

There have been other systematic massacres resulting from deliberately thought out policies, often within the framework of an existing conflict, which are more difficult to define. For example, the 1965 massacres in Indonesia had no ethnic dimension while, on the other hand, the deaths of tens of thousands of people in Sudan could well qualify as genocide. The silent, unwitnessed tragedy of the people of the Nuba mountain area in 1992 has never really been picked up by the media. Yet, in the name of Jihad, the whole population was either massacred or deported to camps in the north of the country, families were split up and many sent into slavery with 'fortunate' children placed in Moslem families as part of the forced Islamisation of the people of Sudan. The repression that was practised by Islamabad when East Pakistan seceded from union with West Pakistan to become Bangladesh was also denounced as genocide. If Rwanda represents the most rapid exodus in history, then that out of Bangladesh was without doubt the largest: within a few months, between nine and ten million people fled to India. However, despite the way in which the West Pakistan forces tried to repress the Bengali people, it is difficult to argue convincingly on ethnic grounds in this case.

The mass killings in Cambodia also enter that category of crimes committed in the pursuit of constructing a new social order from the ashes of the old. Before the madness of the Khmer Rouge was wreaked upon the whole population, intellectuals and people with any kind of formal education were considered enemies. The simple existence of the social and professional groups to which such people belonged were seen as an obstacle to the birth process of the 'New Man'. The term 'autogenocide' has been used in regard to Cambodia, yet this gives the impression that the victims actually killed themselves and is therefore another example of how facts are trivialised and the focus removed from those who are really responsible. But even if French journalist Jean Lacouture could justify saying that 'the Khmer version of national socialism accorded two-thirds of the population the same status as the Jews in fascist Germany',[21] it is clear that the Khmer Rouge never intended the extermination of the Cambodian people, although their actions raised many questions as to their ultimate objective. The guilt of Khmer Rouge leaders has now been properly established, with no extenuating circumstances permitted, yet far too much time was allowed to pass before it was generally admitted that those who first played the role of liberators had in turn become executioners. Many western intellectuals could be accused of complicity in this silent cover-up.

Tibet, where the tragic situation has continued for years with very little outside interest, raises similar questions. In order to bring enlightenment to a reactionary people, so it claimed, China first found it necessary to decimate them. Tibet was then made to suffer tremendously both during the Chinese invasion in 1951 and again during the cultural revolution.

The extermination, whether of a whole people or a tribe of several hundred, is unquestionably genocide. Lemkin postulated that the extermination of any national or ethnic group impoverished humanity as a whole, for our cultural heritage is no less than the total sum of that which every nation and group contributes to it.[22] Therefore, the extermination of an Amazonian tribe represents a loss to the whole human race, even if the intention here is to destroy a culture, rather than to physically obliterate the tribe *per se* from the face of the earth.

Finally, let us turn to Bosnia. Every party involved in the conflict there has committed war crimes, the Serbs certainly on a far greater scale than the Bosnians or Croatians, and certainly they are the only party to have systematically committed crimes against humanity throughout the war. However, they remain crimes against humanity and not genocide. In contradiction to most conflicts since 1945, the objective of the war in Bosnia has been concerned with control over territory rather than over the inhabitants. The Serb's initial objective was to 're-possess' what was considered to be Serbian territory by removing all non-Serbs, but not to annihilate them completely. The strategy of imposing systematic terror, the rapes and the concentration camps have to be seen in this light. Serbs killed Moslems on a large scale because they were Moslems (the Croats were not singled out in the same way, at least not systematically), but their intention was to get rid of the Moslems not to exterminate them. The Serbian camps can be compared to the Nazi concentration camps, such as Dachau or Buchenwald, but certainly not to the extermination camps and factories of death such as Auschwitz or Treblinka. It is sufficiently serious to make an accusation of crimes against humanity but it is unnecessary to add an accusation of genocide for, once again, this only succeeds in trivialising the nature of a genocide. We see what has happened – and continues to happen – in Bosnia as particularly remarkable because it is at the heart of Europe, where Nazism developed and where postwar reconstruction was based on that famous 'Never again!'. It is for that reason that the Bosnian tragedy affects us so deeply and concerns us more than other, and worse, tragedies further afield. But on a universal scale, the crime carried out by the Hutu militias in Rwanda must rate as far more ignominious. To state this is not in any way to diminish the guilt of the Serb leaders and the overall responsibility of the Serbs for the Bosnian conflict.

Raul Hilberg, the American historian, in his authoritative work, *The Destruction of the European Jews*, described four stages in the process which led to their destruction: classification as a Jew, expropriation of property, restriction to ghettos and camps and the removal to concentration camps and eventual extermination.[23] Although the destiny of the Jews was already sealed with the proclamation of the Nuremberg Laws, which defined what it was to be Jewish, the whole process took nine years. If the situation bears any kind of comparison, the Serbs in Bosnia settled for stages two and three, although they achieved in a matter of months what took the Nazis years to accomplish. By a further comparison, the Hutu leaders went from stage one to stage four within just a few days.

Thus, using the definitions of both Lemkin and the Convention, and placing them within the context of the larger category of crimes against humanity in general, there have really only been three genuine examples of genocide during the course of the twentieth century: that of the Armenians by the Young Turks in 1915, that of the Jews and Gypsies by the Nazis and, in 1994, that of the Tutsis by the Hutu racists.

CHAPTER 2

Three Genocides in the Twentieth Century

Three genocides in the twentieth century? There are some who might regard this as an unjustifiably categorical statement that ignores other crimes against humanity targeted at specific populations. The former USSR, for example, committed wholesale slaughter of the Checheno-Ingush, the Crimean Tartars and the Volga Germans during the Second World War. Let us also not forget earlier massacres of Tutsis in Rwanda between 1959 and 1963, in 1973 and since 1990, nor the killings of Hutus by Tutsis and Tutsis by Hutus in Burundi in 1972 and 1988. But, as discussed in the previous chapter, examples such as these are distinguishable in both nature and degree from the three designable genocides.

There are other shameful episodes prior to 1945 which will be mentioned briefly here. During their invasion of China, particularly in the attempted occupation of Nanking, the Japanese were faced with only one real problem: there were too many Chinese. In the Soviet Union, the collectivisation and *dekulakisation* programmes in the Ukraine in the 1930s, which were accompanied by a much higher death rate than elsewhere in the USSR, raises a real problem for history. There certainly is an issue of intentionality here, for Stalin always suspected the Ukraine of harbouring ideas of independence for which he was determined that it should be punished. However, his intention was to punish the region for its resistance to his plans, not to achieve their complete extermination, although this tragic episode of Russian history was on such a scale that it is calculated to have caused the deaths of six million Ukrainians. Most historians would agree that, if required to name the three greatest criminals

21

of this century, Stalin would share equal billing with Hitler and Mao. These three men were responsible for the most horrendous massacres of the last hundred years.

The Young Turks: Territory and Nationalism

The 1915 genocide of the Armenians was carried out by an organisation called Ittihad, or the Young Turks, a reform movement led by Enver and Talaat which sought to spread its 'modern' ideas throughout the Ottoman Empire. There had been an earlier massacre of 300,000 Armenians in 1895 under Sultan Habdul Hamid, but the 1915 massacre was on a very much larger scale: it resulted in the deaths of nearly one million people and brought an end to the Armenian presence in Anatolia. It was also the first time in history that forced deportations were employed as a means of extermination.

There were between 1.5 and 2 million Armenians living in communities across the territory covered by present-day Turkey with the main concentration in northeast Anatolia. The extermination process took the same form everywhere except in Constantinople and Smyrna. It began in February 1915, when the Armenians were disarmed and ousted from the Ottoman army. The first deportations took place two months later. Prominent locals were arrested and able-bodied men were ordered to report immediately to the authorities. When they obeyed the order, in most cases they were killed. Then came the carefully planned deportations from Anatolia to Alep and the Syrian desert. The journey was a living hell. The caravans were constantly attacked by Ottoman police and the local people through whose territory they had to pass. Rape, the splitting-up of families, forced conversions of women to Islam – sometimes the only way to avoid being killed – were all daily experiences for the deportees. In addition, many were taken as slaves. Left without their leaders, their able-bodied men or any weapons, they were defenceless. Those who survived to reach Alep found no arrangements had been made for them and they were sent further on into the desert where their journey finally ended. By mid-1916, the remaining suvivors were sold as slaves. Only 300,000 out of the total Armenian population managed to reach refuge in Russia and no Armenian remained in the eastern provinces.

The massacre is well documented, particularly in the papers of the American ambassador Henri Morgenthau, the research work of historian Alfred Toynbee on behalf of the British government, the witness accounts of Germans living in various regions of Ottoman Turkey and the famous 'secret report' of the German pastor Johannes Lepsius. Paul Thibaut, a French philosopher, has pointed out that whereas some aspects of this genocide were those that have been traditionally associated with the crime, others were quite modern.[1] The ideology of the Young Turk movement and the methods they used to uproot, displace and eventually wipe out the Armenians all belong to the twentieth century. They used such tactics as splitting up the victims by separating the leaders from their people, the strong and able-bodied from the weak and infirm, the women who could be converted, etc., and by imposing constant hardships on the deportees in order to demoralise them. Essential for the success of such massive deportations was guaranteed control over the territories they passed through. For this the Turks depended both on the traditional impenetrable Ottoman bureaucracy and on the new railways which were used wherever they existed. Another well-established method of control was the encouragement given to police and local people to harrass the columns of displaced people and rob them of their possessions.

The objective was clearly not to dominate or to oppress, but to effect a complete extermination of the Armenian people in the Ottoman empire. From May to August 1915, a population of 1.2 million disappeared from the Ottoman territories where they had lived. With the exception of those who succeeded in fleeing to the Russian empire and the communities of Constantinople and Smyrna, all perished. Between 600,000 and one million defenceless Armenians died, representing almost half of the entire Armenian population.[2] Yet there is still controversy as to whether or not there was a genocide. Turkey has always contested this, as have many historians. The orientalist Bernard Lewis recently described it as 'the Armenian version of history'[3] and the survival of Armenian communities in the two large cities has often been used as an argument to prove that there was no genocide. But consideration should be given to the complications involved in trying to remove the Armenian communities from cities where there already existed a large number of foreign residents and potential witnesses. For Gérard Chaliand, co-author of *Génocide des Arméniens*, the objective was to resolve a territorial problem during a period of strong nationalist feeling. It was not simply a question of removing a population suspected of complicity with their enemy, Russia – a theory that has been much discussed – but of using the deportations themselves as the instrument of extermination.[4]

The Young Turks sought to radically transform the economic and social structures of the Ottoman empire. In 1915, under the banner of nationalism, that meant a Turkey that was fully Turkish and Moslem, which necessitated a reduction both in the number of Christians and in the amount of territory they occupied. Therefore the Armenians were very specifically targeted purely and simply as Armenians. Although it deals with an earlier period, Elia Kazan's film, *America, America*, shows how the Greeks, who were also Christian but smaller in number in Anatolia than the Armenian population there, were looked upon differently from the Armenians, although they too were subject to continual harassment. But the deportations of Armenians from the central regions of Anatolia, in any case far from the Russian border, can only be explained as a desire to exterminate them. In twentieth century Balkan states, still partly under Ottoman domination, population displacements have been a frequent occurrence, but never accompanied by killings on such a scale. There is no document that irrefutably confirms the order to carry out the extermination, but then there is no written text from Hitler ordering the Final Solution to the Jewish 'problem'. The debate will therefore continue. But what seems to be the determining factor is that the Armenians were individually condemned to death because they belonged to an identifiable group and the systematic massacres of the children prove that it was not simply the elimination of a present or potential enemy, but also the generation to come.

The Nazis: Industrialised Killing

It was the lack of international reaction to the Armenian genocide that supposedly encouraged Hitler to believe that he could proceed with his Final Solution for the Jews with little or no risk of protest or opposition from other countries. But this – the largest, most cold-blooded and most determinedly methodical genocide of the twentieth century – was not just the work of one man, one party or a single group of fanatics; it depended for its success on the efficiency of the German bureaucracy as a whole.

This has been well documented in two works that should be essential reading for any student of modern history: Raul Hilberg's monumental *The Destruction of the European Jews*, which has already been referred to, and Hannah Arendt's essay, *Eichmann in Jerusalem*.[5] They show clearly how the overall plan to exterminate the Jews was part of a huge bureaucratic process, a mosaic of miniscule fragments, each one individually very ordinary and commonplace: everyday activities such as memos, letters, telegrams and telephone calls, embedded in habit, routine and tradition which were converted into a system of mass destruction. Only a tiny percentage of those who participated in the genocide actually shot a Jew or turned on the gas. It was the bureaucrats who helped to destroy the Jewish people, often whilst remaining seated at their desks, on guard at the entrance to a gas chamber or carrying out a technical job: preparing decrees or posters, organising transport or working out a railway schedule. All of them contributed to one single end: the extermination of the Jews.

This was achieved in stages, each one the result of multiple decisions taken by countless bureaucrats within a vast administrative machinery. The whole procedure evolved step by step in an almost autonomous manner thanks to the zeal of the German civil servants who put themselves at the service of an extermination plan. Raul Hilberg has shown how there were four principal stages, (see Chapter 1), although these did not necessarily correspond to a pre-established order. At first the killings were carried out by mobile teams (the *Einsatzgruppen*) and then later they were concentrated in the death camps for gassing, rather than shooting, which allowed the executioners to remain anonymous from their victims. It was an ingenious system which avoided any one person being directly responsible for an actual killing. The decision to graduate from death trucks to death camps therefore not only indicated a change in the degree of the crime, but also in its nature.

Each stage in the process was faced with problems and a multitude of administrative obstacles that civil servants strove to overcome. By 1933, the Jews had been almost entirely emancipated and integrated into German society. Cutting these links between Jews and 'Germans' proved to be a most complex operation that required all the public services and offices of the German administration to apply anti-Jewish measures at one time or another. These bureaucrats usually brought a remarkable degree of enthusiasm to their task, even volunteering thousands of proposals to increase efficiency or provide a solution to a problem. Every day, inhabitual situations were dealt with by habitual practices. To give one example, the German railways invoiced the security police for transporting the Jews, calculating the costs involved in a one-way trip for each deportee on the basis of the number of kilometres travelled; children travelled for half-price.

Hilberg shows convincingly that the destruction of the Jewish people was not accomplished by putting laws and individual orders into effect, but as a result of a state of mind, of tacit understandings and the smooth synchronisation of tasks. The machinery of destruction impregnated German society, covering all aspects of it in an extremely decentralised manner.

As the system evolved, more complex requirements arose which were met by increasing the involvement of the different services, party offices, commercial enterprises and army sections at all levels. The extermination of the Jews was a total process, comparable in its diversity to modern warfare.

Clearly then, it was not only the Nazis who were responsible for the genocide. Such a large-scale administrative process could not be achieved by any one single organisation. In its structure, the bureaucratic machinery was little different from organised German society as a whole.

As the operation grew in size, civil servants took on larger responsibilities and gradually it became easier to draw up edicts against the Jews which were accepted as having the force of law. Thus, over the years, there was a decrease in the number of laws concerning Jews and instead an increasing number of decrees and edicts were issued, along with a wider scope for applying them. Written orders were replaced by verbal commands with an increasing flexibility in enforcing them. As Hannah Arendt has shown, the crime was carried out by millions of men and women who were neither perverts nor sadists, but frighteningly normal.

It is estimated that 5.1 million Jews died; three million were killed in the death camps, more than 1.3 million were shot by the *Einsatzgruppen* on the Eastern Front and the rest died in the ghettos from hunger and despair.

These were the most directly targeted massacres in recorded history; the most methodical and the most selective carried out by a modern, industrialised society. It had nothing to do with the war, which cannot explain the Nazi enthusiasm for destroying the Jewish people. Auschwitz and the other death camps represent a significant break with history; there was no precedent. Stalin and Mao may have succeeded in killing more people than Hitler but never before – and never again until so very recently – has there been such assembly-line, methodical killing resulting from a system put into effect over a period of years. Never before had there been such a determined effort to target a group defined by purely racial criteria. This was not just the worst pogrom in Jewish history, but by its very nature it was a different crime from all that preceded it. Other genocides and other massacres are not less serious nor can they be any more easily excused, but the Final Solution remains the most singular and exceptional crime with which there is no comparison. Any attempt to put Auschwitz into perspective through attempts at historical revisionism can only be an intellectual fraud.

Hutu Racist Ideology

It took exactly 50 years for Primo Levi's prediction that 'it could all happen again' to be realised. Even if the circumstances of the Jewish genocide are different in regard both to the scale of the killings and in the methods used, *it* or something very like *it* has indeed happened again. Although it is true that previous massacres of Hutus in Burundi and Tutsis in Burundi and Rwanda seemed very like acts of genocide,[6] they were never part of a concerted plan aimed at what might be called a Final Solution to the Tutsis 'problem' in Rwanda (although there are instinctive reservations about making this kind of comparison).

Just as Hitler's grand plan was founded on an engrained European anti-semitism which he played on by singling out the Jews as the source of all Germany's ills, the Hutu radicals are inheritors of the colonial lunacy of classifying and grading different ethnic groups in a racial hierarchy. While the Jews were described by the Nazis as 'vermin', the Tutsis were called *invenzi* ('the cockroaches that have to be crushed'). Anti-Tutsi propaganda presented them as a 'minority, well-off and foreign' – so similar to the image developed to stigmatise the Jews – and thus an ideal scapegoat for all Rwanda's problems. The radicalisation of the Hutu began around 1990, when their monopoly of power was first seriously challenged by the army of the Rwandan Patriotic Front (RPF). This was reinforced by the power-sharing conditions of the 1993 Arusha Accords which offered credible possibilities for national reconciliation and peace for the majority of Rwandans at the expense of the ruling Hutu parties. At that point, the Hutu extremists decided on the relentless pursuit of Tutsis and moderate Hutus.

The plot was devised within the close circle surrounding President Juvénal Habyarimana. From 1990, at the instigation, and with the active complicity of Habyarimana and his government, massacres of Tutsis increased and went unpunished. Two Hutu parties – a wing of the Movement Républican National for development (MRND), 'the only party to have held power since independence, and the Coalition for the Defence of the Republic (CDR), a more recently created, extremist group – increasingly promoted a racist ideology. With the complicity of the army and those in power, they developed a simple strategy for retaining control through the formation of militias and the manipulation of the media, both of which later became tools of the genocide itself.

The militias were set up in order to spread terror. The *Interhamwe* ('those who attack together') and the *Impuzamugambi* ('those who only have one aim'), the youth wings of the MRND and CDR respectively, soon claimed 50,000 members between them. They carried out intimidation raids and 'punitive expeditions' against the terrorized Tutsi population as well as Hutus who supported democracy and negotiations with the RPF. It is not as well-known as it should be that for the previous two or three years an impressive movement in favour of a multi-party system, the rule of law and a respect for human rights had grown up in Rwanda. There were a large number of indidividual initiatives, the monopoly of one-party power had been broached and independent human rights organisations set up. In the eyes of the CDR and MRND these democrats were traitors who only merited the fate of all traitors. Although there were certainly many obstacles, political change seemed inevitable and reconciliation hovered on the horizon, but only at the expense of the racist parties who had the most to lose from them – and everything to gain by preventing them.

Between 1991 and 1994, alarm bells were ringing and signs were there to be read, in the form of massacres that went unpunished. These warning signals were even reported by the UN Human Rights Commission. In 1993 and 1994, thousands of militia members were given arms and military training by the Rwandan Armed Forces (the FAR) which, thanks to French generosity, grew from 5000 to 40,000 men, thus enabling it to take on both the RPF and the internal opposition. In September 1992, a document originating from FAR headquarters established the distinction between the principal enemy and their supporters. The first is defined as:

Tutsis inside the country or outside, extremists and
longing to return to power, who have never recognised
and never will recognise the reality of the 1959 social
revolution [when the Tutsi were thrown out of power],
and who would take back power in Rwanda by any means
possible, including the use of arms.[7]

The second is described as: 'anybody who gives any kind
of support to the main enemy' (the Hutu opposition).

In a country which receives virtually no information from
the outside world, local media, particularly the radio, play
an essential role. For a large part of the population, a
transistor radio is the only source of information and therefore
has the potential for exerting a powerful influence. Rwandan
radio broadcasts are in two languages, French and the
national language, Kinyarwanda, which is spoken by all
Rwandans. Less than a year before the genocide began, two
close associates of President Habyarimana (his brother-in-
law Alphonse Ntimavunda and Félicien Kabuga, a
businessman married to his daughter) set up the 'private'
radio station, popularly known as Radio Mille Collines.
Assured of a large audience thanks to regular programmes
of popular music, the programmes in Kinyarwanda broadcast
unceasing messages of hate, such as 'the grave is only half
full. Who will help us to fill it?'. Christened 'the radio that
kills' by its opponents, it was the basic instrument of
propaganda for the Hutu extremists, and the militias rallied
in support of its slogans.

The monthly journal *Kangura* also contributed to spreading
anti-Tutsi racism. Two months after war broke out in
October 1990, it published a 'Call to the Conscience of the
Bahutu Peoples' accompanied by the 'Ten Bahutu
Commandments'. The eighth of these ten commandments
pronounced, 'The Hutus should stop feeling any pity for the
Tutsis', and the tenth ordered, 'regard as a traitor every Hutu
who has persecuted his brother Hutu for reading, spreading
and teaching this [Hutu] ideology'. Intent on bringing the
ethnic question into the political process, the journal called
for all available means to be used to prevent a successful
conclusion to the negotiations with the RPF. For the racist

Hutu parties, the President had betrayed his people by signing the Arusha Accords, which he had been obliged to accept as a result of international pressure.

On 6 April 1994, the plane carrying President Habyarimana and President Cyprien Ntariyamira of Burundi was shot down by rocket-fire. Although it is not yet known who was behind this assassination, it is clear that it acted as the fuse for the eruption of the violence which led to the greatest tragedy in the history of the country. Even before the national radio station announced the death of the President, death lists were being circulated to facilitate the identification of Hutu opponents, mostly those who supported the democratic movement or promoted human rights. Several ministers in the transition government were assassinated, including members of the democratic opposition such as Prime Minister Agathe Uwilingiyima. These extensive killings veiled the essential fact that although Hutu intellectuals and opponents were being killed, the intention was to systematically eliminate every single Tutsi. As this fundamental distinction was not immediately obvious, neither was it clear at the beginning that a genocide was underway, especially in the growing confusion caused by a new RPF attack.

As the stereotypes of physical characteristics do not always provide sufficient identification – and can even be totally misleading – it was the identity cards demanded at the roadblocks set up by the militias that acted as the signature on a death warrant for the Tutsis. As control of the road could not alone ensure that no Tutsi escaped, the militia leaders divided up the territory under their control so that one man was allocated for every ten households in order to systematically search for Tutsis in their immediate localities. In this way every Tutsi family could be denounced by somebody who knew the members personally: pupils were killed by their teachers, shop owners by their customers, neighbour killed neighbour and husbands killed wives in order to save them from a more terrible death. Churches where Tutsis sought sanctuary were particular targets and the scene of some of the worst massacres: 2800 people in Kibungo, 6000 in Cyahinda, 4000 in Kibeho, to give just a few examples. In Rwanda, the children of mixed marriages take the ethnic group of the father and, although many of the Hutu killers – including some militia leaders – had Tutsi mothers, so effective was the indoctrination programme, that even this apparently counted for nothing. Radio Mille Collines encouraged the violence with statements such as that made at the end of April 1994, 'By 5 May, the country must be completely cleansed of Tutsis.' Even the children were targeted: 'We will not repeat the mistake of 1959. The children must be killed too.' The media directly influenced Hutu peasants, convincing them that they were under threat and encouraging them to 'make the Tutsis smaller' by decapitating them. In the northern areas occupied by the RPF, the peasants were astonished that the Tutsi soldiers did not have horns, tails and eyes that shone in the dark as they had been described in radio programmes.

The genocide spread rapidly to cover the whole country under the control of the government army. By the end of April, it was estimated that 100,000 people had been killed. Africa had never known massacres on such a scale, yet the world was blind to the reality of events. Reviewing headlines in the French and English language press in those first weeks, there is a clear attempt to present the massacres as part of a civil war: 'Rwanda on Fire', 'Fierce Clashes', 'Slaughter', 'Massacre', 'Civil War', 'Bloody Horror', 'Rwanda Anarchy', 'Fall of Kigali Imminent'. It is rare to find a newspaper that made a distinction between the assassinations of specifically targeted Hutus and the systematic elimination of all Tutsis. It took three weeks from 6 April – a long time in the world of CNN-style news – before editorials finally began comparing the situation in Rwanda with Germany under Nazism and referring to it as a genocide.[8] Overall, however, the word genocide rarely appeared in the main headlines – certainly not often enough to raise the awareness of the general public to the extraordinary event that was taking place. Conversely, 'genocide' and 'Holocaust' were frequently and quite incorrectly applied, even by the most widely respected journalists, in reference to the subsequent cholera epidemic in Goma.

Most commentators in the written press highlighted the political objectives of the crime and resisted the temptation to treat the situation as a 'tribal conflict', as if Hutu and Tutsi were two sides of the same coin. But therein lies both a contradiction and a problem: if the aims were political and not tribal in any way, there was, nonetheless, a clear intention to exterminate a group of people on the basis of their ethnic identity. It was not easy to identify what was at stake here, particularly when those who misused the word genocide were, blinded by the extent of the carnage, unable to recognise the characteristic intentionality of the crime.

There are aspects of this genocide which are new and contemporary; others we have seen before. The use of propaganda, the way control was exercised over the population via the militias, the use of the machinery of local administration: these are all reflections of the modern era. So too are the extreme racist ideology and the radical determination to exterminate all Tutsis in one all-encompassing blow. It would be a mistake to think that the killings were carried out in an anarchic manner: the reality is that they were meticulously well organised. However, the means used to accomplish them were primitive in the extreme: for example, the use of machetes and *unfunis*, (wooden clubs studded with metal spikes). Unfortunately, the media eclipsed the first aspect in its preoccupation with the second.

Characteristics of Genocide

All the twentieth-century genocides that we are dealing with here have certain characteristics in common.

First, the consequence of a genocide always reaches beyond the target group and the country where it took place – where it leaves deep scars on the national psyche. The psychologist Leo Alexander has described how 'very violent and deep-rooted destructive urges cannot be limited or confined to a single object, but must inevitably expand and turn against the group to which the individual belongs, then finally against himself'.[9] The Hutu killers turned against fellow Hutus who tried to save Tutsis and the vast majority of Hutus abandoned their homes and fled the country as a result of propoganda-inspired fear of the RPF. Huge population displacements, whether as a result of force or out of fear of persecution, are typical of all three genocides this century. And none of the three regimes that perpetrated genocide survived military defeat.

Second, the crime of genocide, as with other crimes against humanity that target ethnic or religious groups, is often accompanied by savage cruelty. It seems paradoxical that out of 'humanitarian concern' for the mental wellbeing of their soldiers at a time when each member of an *Einsatzgruppen* could be called upon to kill several hundred people every day, the Nazis decided to industrialise the killings by building gas chambers.

Third, genocide has to be a collective act. Although some of the killings may be one individual killing another, the logic remains that of the collective act and most of the slaughter is carried out by several people together, on almost every occasion resulting in several victims. The instigators of a genocide impose an obligation to kill on those who carry out their orders. Obedience helps to foster a feeling of belonging to the group and diminishes any feeling of guilt. It effectively dehumanises the killers who find a certain solidarity in their actions. The soldiers of the *Einsatzgruppen* were not chosen by a specialised selection process but were 'normal, ordinary' people who quickly developed a taste for killing. How many Hutu peasants learned to take pleasure from killing their neighbours and were swept away by the feeling of power which results from taking part in a collective crime? Why did Hutus who had protected Tutsis whom they knew personally then join up with bands of killers in other villages?[10] Hannah Arendt has shown that the Final Solution, although designed by a very small group close to Hitler, was actually effected by an enormous number of ordinary people who were convinced that it was 'them or us'. Statements such as Himmler's, 'If we do not carry out this task now, the Jewish people will eventually destroy the German people'[11] encouraged this fear. Radio Mille Collines made similar statements against the Tutsis.

International indifference is a characteristic of all three cases of genocide this century, although the world knew, or at least had the possibility to know, what was happening and yet chose not to take a stand. With regard to Armenia, the French, British and Russian governments did nothing beyond making softly-worded official protests. During the Second World War, at no time did the Allies modify their military objectives in order to save Jews, even after 1944 when there was no longer any possible doubt as to what was happening. Half a million Jews were murdered in Auschwitz between March and November 1944, when the last gassings took place, yet the railway lines leading to the death camps were never targeted. And the world remained silent in the face of the genocide of the Tutsis in 1994. American civil servants were even ordered not to use the word to describe what was happening – despite (or perhaps because of) a UN convention that obliges its signatories to take action to prevent genocide.

Finally, the victim has to be identified; the first step in any genocide. It was not difficult to define the Armenians, a Christian minority in an almost totally Moslem country that can be seen now as a nation in embryo. It was harder to define the German Jews: the problem was never totally resolved, despite the Nuremberg Laws by which the Germans constructed a complex system of categories. Theoretically, it was more straightforward to define a Tutsi: ethnic identity was inherited from the father, regardless of the origins of the mother, and this had to be registered on the obligatory identity cards. How can it have been possible that the lives of hundreds of thousands of people were decided in no more than the time it took to check one of those identity cards?

CHAPTER 3

The Hutu and the Tutsi

For those with no specialised knowledge of the region, it is perhaps not easy to understand the issues of ethnicity in Rwanda: the ongoing debates appear to have political overtones.[1] This demonstrates how complex the question is and how little is really known about the origin of the terms Hutu and Tutsi. In African societies with a pre-colonial oral tradition, there is of course no way the answers to such questions can be proven scientifically. An unbiased reading of the available literature, however, would seem to indicate that the respective authors are in agreement more often perhaps than they would be willing to admit.

One thing is certain, the massacres in Rwanda are not the result of a deep-rooted and ancient hatred between two ethnic groups. In fact, the Hutu and Tutsi cannot even correctly be described as ethnic groups for they both speak the same language and respect the same traditions and taboos. It would be extremely difficult to find any kind of cultural or folkloric custom that was specifically Hutu or Tutsi. There were certainly distinguishable social categories in existence before the arrival of the colonisers, but the differences between them were not based on ethnic or racial divisions. It was by exaggerating such stereotypes and supporting one group against the other that the colonisers reinforced, consolidated and ultimately exacerbated such categorising. After independence, each time the party in power searched for a way out of political difficulty, it played the ethnic card. However, it is true that Hutu–Tutsi antagonism has since become absorbed by the people themselves, even if it does not really correspond to an anthropological distinction, and is therefore politically relevant. Jean-Pierre Chrétien describes the phenomenon as 'tribalism without tribes'.[2]

Colonial Categories: 'White-Coloureds' and 'Negroes'

Nobody really knows the exact origin of the Hutu, Tutsi and Twa peoples (the Twa represent only 1 per cent of the population and have never played a significant role in the region). The three groups speak the same language, share the same territory and follow the same traditions. By all definitions, this should qualify Rwanda as a nation in the true sense. The different groups acknowledged the same Tutsi king (the Mwami), considered to be of divine origin and responsible for fertility. This monarchy was the result of numerous battles and amalgamations between the many small kingdoms and fiefs, some Hutu and some Tutsi.

At the beginning of the twentieth century, the various groups could have best been described as castes within a hierarchy maintained by practising endogamy. Intermarriage was not actually forbidden but, nevertheless, was very much disapproved of. In Rwanda, children of mixed marriages have always been attributed the ethnic group of their father. Social distinctions corresponded to a division of tasks: the Tutsi mainly occupied with cattle raising and the Hutu working the land as farmers.

Although there are socio-cultural differences between the groups, many integrating factors kept them together. For example, territory was not split into distinct ethnic areas; mixed marriages could take place; and war was waged in common against neighbouring kingdoms. Until the colonisers arrived, society in Africa was comprised of identifiable categories, separate social classes or castes that differed in regard to the amount of power each could exercise. As a result of migrations at different times, there are even some examples of 'new' ethnic groups being created, for example, the Banyarwanda in Uganda and Zaire.

The first Europeans to reach Rwandan territory described the people and their way of life in terms very much influenced by the scientific ideas of their time. Until the beginning of the nineteenth century, the origin of Africa's many peoples was regarded by Europeans as rooted in the biblical story of Ham, Noah's son. The book of Genesis tells how Ham and his descendants were cursed throughout all generations after he had seen his father naked. The 'Blacks' were believed to be descendants of Ham, their colour a result of that curse. At the beginning of the nineteenth century, linguistic studies, archaeological research and rational thinking led to a questioning of this theory, which was subsequently replaced with a system of classifying people according to their physical characteristics: skin colour, type of hair, shape of the skull, etc. Those who were then classified as 'Blacks' were regarded as 'another' kind of human being, not descended from Noah. Yet this classification did not cover the whole population of the African continent. Explorers in the region we now know as Niger and in the areas of the Zambezi and the Upper Nile, came across people that did not correspond to the caricature of the negro.

So it was that German, and later Belgian, colonisers developed a system of categories for different 'tribes' that was largely a function of aesthetic impressions. Individuals were categorised as Hutu or Tutsi according to their degree of beauty, their pride, intelligence and political organisation. The colonisers established a distinction between those who did not correspond to the stereotype of a negro (the Tutsi) and those who did (the Hutu). The first group, 'superior Africans', were designated Hamites or 'white coloureds' who represented a 'missing link' between the 'Whites' and the 'Blacks'. Also included in this group were the Galla peoples of Ethiopia and Somalia. 'Any quality attributed to an African group must be read as a sign of interbreeding with "non-negro" cultures':[3] this 'hamitic' ideology translates into the hypothesis, for which there is no serious proof, that a migration of the Galla took place in the seventeenth century, thus explaining the similarities between the Galla and the Tutsi.[4]

This theory protects the church's claim that all the peoples of the earth originate from Noah and also corresponds with the thesis of Joseph Arthur Gobineau that was popular at the time. In his book, *Essai sur l'inégalité des races humaines*, Gobineau stated that racial superiority was dependent on observable physical and therefore 'objective' criteria. For him, the 'Hamites' descended from the first 'white' excursions into

Africa and degeneration took place as a result of inter-breeding.[5]

Although lacking proof, successive colonial administrators and missionaries became convinced that the Tutsi were immigrants to the region and that these cattle owners were of different genetic stock to the Hutu. Jean-Pierre Chrétien and Filip Reyntjens have both written of how the Tutsi were considered as 'Hamites', coming from a 'superior race' or as 'Aryans' or as 'Europeans under a black skin'.[6] J. Sasserath, a Belgian doctor, described them in 1948: 'The Hamites are 1.90 metres tall. They are slim. They have straight noses, high foreheads, thin lips. The Hamites seem distant, reserved, polite and refined.'[7]

According to this theory, the Hutu (the majority of the population) are assimilated to the Bantu. Although first used to describe a linguistic group, the term Bantu rapidly took on a pejorative racial connotation to designate the 'negroes' as members of another human species who played the role of serfs within society. According to Dr Sasserath: 'The rest of the population is Bantu. ... possessing all the characteristics of the negro: flat noses, thick lips, low foreheads, brachycephalic skulls. They are like children, shy and lazy and usually dirty.'[8]

The Twa, a small minority of pygmies who live off hunting and foraging in the forests, are the only really endogamous group and are regarded as inferiors by both Hutu and Tutsi. They were denigrated by the colonisers: Count Von Götzen, the first European on Rwandan soil, declared them 'a caste of dwarfs'. The Twa keep themselves apart and are treated with contempt by the rest of population.

The colonisers also justified making distinctions between Hutu and Tutsi on the basis of their different political and social organisation, considering the Tutsi's to be superior to that of the Hutu. Through the custom of *ubuhake*, the right to own cattle, which was transmitted from father to son, Tutsi domination was effectively assured. The Mwami was ultimate owner of all the cattle which he allocated to individuals who could in turn pass them on to others. The chief, usually Tutsi, demanded labour and agricultural produce in return for protection. This system, often described as feudal, did not imply a servant–master relationship, but rather one of cattle owner and farmer. When the evolutionary and racial theories were in vogue at the beginning of this century, the phenomena of different social class was interpreted in racial terms and contributed to this habit of compartmentalising Rwandan society. Power was in the hands of the Tutsi pasturalists and hard labour was the lot of the agriculturalists, the 'Hutu negroes' and the Twa. In reality, the division of tasks was never that rigid and occasionally a less well-off Tutsi cattle owner might agree to marry his daughter to a rich Hutu farmer. As a result, the term 'Tutsi' became synonymous with a rise in social position.

Promoting the Tutsi

The Germans, who never established a large presence in Rwanda – in 1914, there were only five civil servants covering the whole country – supported the 'superior race' theory. They applied a policy of indirect control through military assistance to the Tutsi to allow them to take over the last remaining independent kingdoms. The Tutsi dynasty had made significant conquests in the interior since the end of the seventeenth century, eliminating the Hutu kings and chiefs one by one and no doubt thereby stirring-up tensions between castes.

Determined to practice a policy based on this racial theory, which was seen as no more than the 'reality' of the situation, it was the Belgians who then reorganised customary relations between the Tutsi lords and Hutu serfs by introducing chiefdoms and sub-chiefdoms to reinforce Tutsi domination. These administrative reforms, which took place during the 1930s, were used to depose most of the Hutu chiefs. The result was that in 1959, 43 of the 45 chiefdoms and 549 of the 559 sub-chiefdoms were under the control of Tutsis. It was at this time that identity cards were progressively introduced.

The Roman Catholic Vicar Apostolic of Rwanda, who stated that 'the greatest harm that the Belgian government could do to itself and to the country would be to suppress the Tutsi caste', was influential in the decision to give preference to the Tutsis. In 1927, a letter from the Belgian Resident recommended official recognition that the best hope for Rwanda's future lay with the Tutsi for as 'born leaders, they have a natural ability to command'. He claimed that this was also acknowledged by the Hutu themselves.[9]

The Belgians also favoured the Tutsi students and the main priority of Rwanda's schools was their education. As this was, inevitably, also the policy at tertiary level, the educated elite at the country's university, Astrida, the future administrative and technical backbone of the country, were very largely Tutsi. The colonisers blamed the imbalance in the schools and resulting low social standing of the Hutu on Hutu passivity making no acknowledgement of their own role in the situation. The legacy of this theory continues even today. Omer Marchal, the Belgian author, wrote in 1994 that in the colonial period, 'The majority of the Tutsi could read, but did not want to vote. The Hutu would all have liked to vote, but only a minority could read. This is the fault of their parents who regarded school as useless, while the Tutsi pushed to have their children educated.'[10]

The missionaries also supported the Tutsi power structure, using it to evangelise from the top down. The Tutsi chiefs, once they had become Christian, then felt a moral obligation to convert the Hutu masses. The seminaries were more open to the Hutu than the schools. Moreover, while seeming to support the monarchy, the colonial administration emptied it of any real meaning and legitimacy. The colonisers presumed that Rwandans would come to accept the Catholic church in this role as they were gradually converted to Christianity and the influence of the church consequently increased.

Thus, in short, if the categories of Hutu and Tutsi were not actually invented by the colonisers, the policies practised by the Germans and Belgians only served to exacerbate them. They played an essential role in creating an ethnic split and ensured that the important feeling of belonging to a social group was fuelled by ethnic, indeed racial, hatred.

The Belgian About-Turn and the 1959 Revolution

There was growing social confrontation during the 1950s accompanied by the radicalisation of the younger generation, both Hutu and Tutsi, who absorbed this colonial analysis of the ethnic situation and then adopted it as their own. Although, after 1959, the educated Tutsi sometimes backed the theory of the mono-ethnic origins of the population following the removal from power of the Tutsi aristocracy – which was particularly sensitive to pseudo-scientific proof of its superior qualities, according to some historians – the myth of Egyptian origins and Hamitic superiority was supported by many among the Tutsi people. Some Hutu discovered the extent to which they, the 'native' people of the region, had been 'despoiled' and developed their own theory of the 'Ethiopian invaders', categorising the Tutsi as colonisers, the same as the Belgians. Thus, by the end of the 1950s, an ethnic awareness had certainly developed among the Rwandan elite. This confusion of a social problem with an ethnic problem during the period leading up to independence was attested to in an important document produced in 1957 by nine Hutu intellectuals, the *Bahutu Manifesto*. The sub-title, *A note on the social aspects of the indigenous racial problem in Rwanda*, is significant in itself. It is an expression of the first open opposition to Tutsi domination, drawing its inspiration from democratic and egalitarian ideas. It seems to be more a plea for democracy than a call to revolution although it does contain a denunciation of 'colonialism by the Hamites [Tutsis] over the Hutu'.[11]

It was the first generation of Hutu intellectuals, educated in the seminaries but excluded from a role in the administration of the country, who rallied under the banner of ethnic separatism. They found support for their protest among the new generation of missionaries who were inspired by a 'Christian socialism' based on the fashionable ideas of equality, democracy and social progress. This encouraged the Hutu protest movement to base itself around the Catholic church. Rwanda was a model of colonial Christianity with almost 65 per cent of the population converted.

When the first representative councils were set up at each level of the administrative structure from 1952 onwards, the Hutu were in a position to establish a strong presence by force of superior numbers. This position was further reinforced in 1959, when the Belgian administration decided that it would from now on support the educated Hutu rather than the Tutsi, now referred to as 'feudal colonists'.

In fact, in the context of a rising tide of African nationalism and a general retreat from the continent by the colonial powers, the Tutsi, deprived of their religious authority, began to question the power of the church and the Belgian authorities. Let down by the Tutsi 'Christian aristocracy' that they had cultivated, church leaders and missionaries suddenly began to embrace republican ideas and supported Hutu emancipation. The arrival of a new Swiss bishop, Monseigneur Perraudin, himself very sensitive to Christian socialist ideas, was an additional boost to the Hutu cause. At this time the country was in the grip of repeated attacks by the *Parmehutu* (the political party promoting Hutu emancipation) against the monarchy and the existing structure of social organisation that exclusively advantaged the Tutsi. Rwandan Tutsis were from now on treated as immigrants and the 1959 'revolutionaries' called for 'the return to Ethiopia of the Tutsi colonisers'. The Hutu had begun to believe that they alone were the native people of Rwanda.

Belgium, criticised at the UN for a colonial policy that ensured that only a handful of the local population in their colonies received sufficient training for them to eventually be promoted to the higher levels of their national administrations – a policy aimed at ensuring that they would not think they were capable of running their own country – gradually ceded power to the small Hutu elite. The democratic principle of majority rule was cited as justification for the removal of the Tutsi from their previous positions of influence; a complete reversal of previous political policy. The Hutu became the 'good guys' who 'have been dominated for so long by the Tutsi' and the Belgians now expressed 'sympathy for the cause of the suppressed masses'.[12]

In 1959, a series of riots directed against the authority of the Tutsi chiefs were allowed by the Belgians to escalate into a revolution accompanied by massacres which killed more than 20,000 Tutsi. These were mainly educated Tutsi killed by the Hutu majority grouped under the banner of the *Parmehutu* and well aware that their superior numbers gave them the upper hand. The 1959 revolution represented a turning point in the political history of Rwanda. It led to the exile of a large number of Tutsi, the exclusion of all Tutsi from the political life of the country and a growing authoritarianism practised by a Hutu power base that was becoming increasingly centralised. Independence was declared in 1962, with the Hutu monopolising power in the country. There were further massacres of Tutsis the following year and growing violence resulting from Hutu determination to play the ethnic card. From this point on, the Tutsi minority became the scapegoat in every political crisis.

The Tutsi as Scapegoat

After a period of calm during which there was an increase in the number of mixed marriages, the ethnic question became more accute at the beginning of the 1970s under the rule of President Kayibanda. A quota was imposed on the Tutsi who were allotted only 10 per cent of the places in the schools and universities and in civil service posts. Unemployment meant fierce competition for jobs among the educated elite. The economic situation contributed to a further radicalisation, although the racial tensions that were so marked among students and the Hutu elite fighting for jobs in an atmosphere of nepotism, barely touched the peasantry in the countryside. Claudine Vidal summed up the situation:

> The Rwandan civil wars demonstrate in an exemplary way the cultural dimension of ethnic politics. The most determined and violent adversaries come from the ranks of the better educated in the population who are more capable of exploiting their knowledge to increase their wealth and obtain the new jobs [resulting from the development process].[13]

Kayibanda's regime continued the practice of listing racial group membership on identity cards. He was able to make use of this in a campaign against the Tutsi, aimed at uniting the Hutu in his support, that targeted 'hybrid' mixed marriages. This was not a general anti-Tutsi offensive, however, but was aimed at those who had modern educational qualifications. After Kayibanda was overthrown by

Juvénal Habyarimana in 1973, there was a period of calm for several years with no massacres at all between 1973 and 1990. But despite this apparent period of appeasement, the ethnic question remained very much alive. Fear was the radicalising element in the caste conflict, each ethnic group guarding the memory of members who were killed in massacres. The country faced further splits with divisions between the north and the south of the country depending on where the different presidents originated. Kayibanda, who came from Gitarama in the south, tended to favour the central and southern regions while Habyarimana, who came from the north, promoted northern areas and accused the southerners of complicity with the Tutsi, who were more numerous in the centre and south of the country. This further rivalry between northern and southern Hutus served to increase political tension in the period up to the RPF guerrilla attacks in 1990.

In that year, the economic situation, which up until then had been relatively good in comparison with neighbouring countries, deteriorated in the wake of plummeting coffee prices and bad weather that meant that large parts of the country suffered food shortages. During the summer of 1990, President Habyarimana was confronted with a protest movement calling for democratic reform. A legally-constituted opposition had been forming in Rwanda following President Mitterrand's call on African countries to open up to the democratic process during a conference in La Baule that summer, and showing that he was prepared to put pressure on francophone African countries in order to achieve this. In addition, the Tutsi diaspora, spread over neighbouring countries in the wake of the pogroms over the years, had begun to organise itself. In Uganda, it formed the Rwandan Patriotic Front (RPF) which gave considerable support to President Museveni in his struggle for power. But many Hutus regarded the Ugandan Tutsis as the descendants of the 'Tutsi aristocracy' that had fled Rwanda in 1959, as many of them had been born outside the country. They had little or no personal knowledge of Rwanda and they spoke English rather than French. They claimed, however, that they were also a part of the Rwandan nation and demanded the right to return home. The RPF always took care to include Hutus within its ranks and avoided presenting an image of an exclusively Tutsi party.[14] The refugees continued to put pressure on Habyarimana to negotiate with them and he eventually agreed, reluctantly, to the setting-up of a national committee to 'identify what the concept of democracy signifies for the majority of the Rwandan people', to define a 'national political charter' and to work out a draft constitution. But on 1 October 1990, the *Inkotanyi* ('those who fight courageously') units of the RPF launched an offensive from Uganda. Although its objective seemed to be limited to presenting an alternative to the regime of President Habyarimana, the invasion was perceived as an attempt to return the Tutsi to power. Its initial effect was to aggravate ethnic tension and unite many Hutus around the President. Habyarimana then incited a series of pogroms against the Tutsi and opposition Hutus, which he justified by calling it the self-defence of the Hutu people against the threat from the feudal Tutsi. This succeeded in reawakening the intense latent mistrust between the two groups.

Habyarimana's regime then shifted their planned programme into a higher gear. At the beginning of 1991, more than 1200 Bagogwe, a clan stemming from the Tutsi, were massacred in the northwest of the country during reprisals carried out by armed militia close to the government. In March 1992, in the region of Bugesera in the south, Hutus carried out a series of attacks on the Tutsis, killing around 300 of them. At the beginning of 1993, 300 civilians, mainly Tutsi, were killed by Hutu militants in the north of the country. When combat was renewed between the RPF and the government forces, hundreds of thousands of Rwandans fled the country. On 4 August 1993, the Arusha Accords were signed in Tanzania, where all the concerned parties were taking part in negotiations aimed at reconciliation and the establishment of democracy in Rwanda. Provision was made for a transitional government to include members of the RPF and the deployment of an international force to supervise their application (the UN Assistance Mission for Rwanda, UNAMIR). But resistance by President Habyarimana and the extremist Hutu parties, as well as the effects of the ethnic tensions in Burundi, succeeded in delaying the implementation of the Accords.

In conclusion, what happened in Rwanda illustrates a situation where the coexistence of different social groups or castes metamorphosed into an ethnic problem with an overwhelmingly racist dimension. The caricature of physical stereotypes, although they did not always hold true and were probably due to the principle of endogamy practised by each group despite the number of mixed marriages, was manipulated to provide proof of the racial superiority of one group over the other. Archaic political divisions were progressively transformed into racial ideologies and repeated outbreaks of violence resulting from the colonial heritage which was absorbed by local elites who then brought it into the political arena. The present generation has internalised this ethnological colonial model, with some groups deliberately choosing to play the tribal card. The regimes that have ruled Rwanda and Burundi since independence have shown that they actually *need* ethnic divisions in order both to reinforce and justify their positions.[15] Finally, however, it was the ethnic classification registered on identity cards introduced by the Belgians that served as the basic instrument for the genocide of the Tutsi people who were 'guilty' on three counts: they were a minority, they were a reminder of a feudal system and they were regarded as colonisers in their own country.

CHAPTER 4

From Indifference to Compassion

Throughout the Rwandan crisis the United Nations, and the principal countries concerned, reacted too late and inconsistently. The international community barely realised that it was confronted with a repeat of a singular crime unknown since the Second World War. Haunted by the ghost of the recent conflict in Somalia, the United States and the Security Council abandoned the Tutsi. And when they finally did decide to take action, it was under the ambiguous banner of humanitarianism that pushed the genocide into the background as universal shock, horror and compassion moved the refugees in the cholera-stricken camps to centre stage.

When the massacres began in Kigali, the western world appeared concerned only for the fate of its own nationals. Within a few days, French and Belgian troops had evacuated almost every white person from Rwanda. Technically speaking, this was a successful operation that relieved the fears of the general public, especially in Belgium where there had been horror and outrage at the killing of ten of their Blue Helmets shortly after the massacres began. With very rare exceptions, the UN agencies, the embassies and non-governmental agencies did not evacuate their local personnel. Throughout the world people watched film of armed soldiers helping to save their compatriots. Those same soldiers were ordered to turn their backs on women and children being slaughtered by adolescents armed only with machetes and sticks. Rarely has there been an episode in history when differences in the status and destiny of groups of human beings has been so obvious. The UN called half-heartedly for a ceasefire before pulling out the main body of UNAMIR troops, reducing them from 2500 to 270 men. The international feeling of relief at that point was both legitimate in respect of those non-Rwandan lives saved but shameful in view of the vast numbers of Rwandans left to their fate in what was being described as a 'senseless tribal struggle'. While the genocide was reaching its peak, apart from a few totally powerless UN troops, there were only a handful of foreigners left in the country.

The Shadow of Somalia

Day-by-day, as the death toll increased, the reality that a genocide was underway became clearer. By the end of April, it was estimated that 100,000 people had been killed, by mid-May 200,000, and by the end of May half a million. Although nobody really knew the actual death toll, the signs of massacres were everywhere and the River Nyaborongo carried thousands of corpses towards Lake Victoria along what Hutu propaganda described as 'the shortest way back to Ethiopia'. But emotions are not easily aroused for the suffering of victims that cannot be seen on our television screens. This was the time when action should have been taken: a military operation was needed to protect the Tutsi, sheltering in their thousands in well identified places such as churches, hospitals and stadia. An intervention at this stage could have saved thousands, if not tens of thousands, of human lives.

But since events in Iraq, Somalia and even Bosnia, no international action can be taken without the leading role of the United States who, this time, were unwilling to act as police force to the world. In Somalia 30 American soldiers died: fewer than the number of New York taxi drivers murdered every year. However, this was a crucial factor in the formulation of new American policy on UN operations, signed by President Clinton just before the beginning of the crisis in Rwanda, which was to serve as a test for this new presidential decision directive (PDD).[1] The PDD clearly signified an abrupt end to any new initiatives on Rwanda, which would be impossible to implement now without American agreement. As far as the Clinton administration was concerned, the United States had to begin to refuse some of the many demands made on it by the UN. In real terms, such a refusal would take the form of imposing draconian conditions on any new operation. The PDD trapped the UN in a vicious circle: the United States would refuse any new deployment of UN Blue Helmets unless all the necessary conditions (logistical, financial, troop deployments, etc.) were fulfilled – yet they could never be fulfilled *without* the active support of the superpower. This Catch 22 situation was further complicated by the added condition that if America was to be involved in any such operations they must have a direct bearing on US national interests. Clearly this was not the case with Rwanda. The real motive behind PDD was a determination to progressively reduce the amount that the United States was contributing to peacekeeping operations, which stood at 30 per cent of the total budget.

The unfortunate Tutsi were the first victims of this new policy. As Richard Dowden of Britain's *Independent* newspaper expressed it, this was the victory of a 'poker mentality. Problem: Somalia. Response: intervention. Result: failure. Conclusion: no more intervention'.[2] As a result, the United States blocked the adoption of any firm resolution for action by the UN and refused to agree to resolution 719 of 17 May 1994, authorising the deployment of a maximum of 5500 men, until it had ensured that there was no risk of any real American commitment. No matter what happened, UN soldiers were not authorised to use force in an attempt to end the massacres. As a result, the text that was finally adopted was worthless. Finally, the Security Council refused to qualify the massacres as the genocide it really was in any of its official papers, as this would have obliged them to intervene under international law. They preferred instead to continue to work towards a ceasefire between the 'parties', thus putting the perpetrators of the genocide and the RPF on an equal footing and thus remaining neutral in the face of a genocide. Fortunately, although it was far too late for hundreds of thousands of Tutsi, the RPF succeeded in winning the war. If the victims of the genocide had received some kind of moral revenge, it was not due to action by the UN or the major powers. It is worth noting that Rwanda had a seat on the UN Security Council at this time which gave its ambassador, a product of the Habyarimana regime, every possible chance to openly express his racist philosophy before its members. Until the French intervention, there was no concrete international action beyond what can only be considered as a gesture by the Human Rights Commission, despite the remarkable work done by its Special Rapporteur, René Degni-Ségui, who made a clear distinction between the genocide of the Tutsi people and the assassinations of individual Hutus.

Throughout this first phase, the tragic events in Somalia, where 18,000 UN troops were still stationed in May 1994, remained a potent memory for the UN Security Council, although the Hutu militias could in no way be compared to the Somali warlords and the histories of the two countries are quite different. Rwanda had neither the same tradition of violence nor the same social structure as Somalia.

There were two things the UN could have done, neither of which it did: it could have made a selective intervention to protect the hospitals, schools and other places where the Tutsi were desperately seeking refuge and it could have clearly recognised the RPF as the legitimate government of Rwanda and so broken off relations with the government that had initiated the genocide. Such measures would have changed the course of Rwanda's history. However, the decision in favour of non-involvement was taken: not at the UN in New York but in the White House in Washington, haunted by the memory of Somalia.

French Intervention: Atonement for the Past?

It was nearly two months after the beginning of the genocide before France, claiming that it had 'a duty to intervene', announced that it was ready to mount an operation in Rwanda. This proposal was greeted with some scepticism, for although France was undoubtedly well placed to intervene from a technical point of view, politically and morally the situation was much more ambiguous.

The French had remained silent in the face of the flagrantly racist policies and practises of the Habyarimana government for far longer than any other country. French authorities had refused to admit that the Rwandan president had become the biggest obstacle to national reconciliation and was using ethnic tactics in order to stay in power. Although Belgium had put an end to military cooperation and considerably reduced its non-military assistance, France did the exact opposite and tripled its aid from 1990.

One month after the RPF offensive in October 1990, Belgium intervened to protect, and subsequently evacuate, its nationals and then withdrew all military troops. France, on the other hand, decided to remain and its troops took an increasingly active role in field combat. According to several sources, French intervention was the determining role in stopping the RPF advances in 1992 and in February 1993. With each new RPF offensive, France increased the number of its troops until they totalled 700 soldiers of the elite Rapid Action Force. France also increased arms deliveries out of all proportion to the actual military situation and the defence needs of the country. The French government had no official defence agreement with Rwanda beyond a basic undertaking, signed in 1975, to provide military assistance. In 1993, Rwanda, a tiny country with a population of seven million, was receiving 55 million French francs (or $10 million) of military aid annually, placing it sixth on the list of African countries receiving such aid (after Cameroon, Central African Republic, Ivory Coast, Djibouti, Gabon and Senegal).

The French decision to intervene was also questionable politically. While France had previously supported 'the negotiation and democratisation process', in contrast to other countries its government remained silent on human rights violations in Rwanda. French involvement in a region which represented practically no strategic interest most likely resulted from a combination of historic links with Africa in general, a concern to maintain an area of francophone influence in the face of what was seen as an expanding anglophone influence and, in keeping with the unorthodox rules that govern the links between France and the countries it fosters, personal relationships between French politicians and businessmen and individual African leaders. It was only at the end of 1993, with the arrival of the UNAMIR troops, that France ceased military support, which it had always justified with the official line that the 'French umbrella' assured worse violence did not take place. Today, we can measure the consequences of that 'enlightened' policy. After the RPF attack in 1990, France became both the main supporter of the regime and the last bastion for President Mabyarimana – a president who continued to reject democracy for Rwanda despite the growing pressure from his internal opposition and the force of international opinion.

However, despite its history, it must be said that France was the only country to attempt any kind of intervention, although François Mitterrand, Edouard Balladur and Alain Juppé were all convinced that they had more to lose than to gain. In fact, French intervention was in an ambiguous position from the very start, regarding the legitimacy of its actions as well as its objectives. The French government sought to legitimise its actions by seeking the authorisation of the Security Council, from which it received the go ahead for Operation Turquoise on 22 June 1994. The purely humanitarian format of the operation, which was to be conducted in a neutral and impartial manner, was strongly emphasised in the Security Council's resolution. This raised the question of the real objectives of the intervention, for it was obvious that the problem itself was not humanitarian. Médecins Sans Frontières pulled no punches when it headlined a press campaign in France with 'Genocide Cannot Be Stopped by Doctors'. Contradictory statements by different members of the government and the actual military action in the field ensured that this ambiguity was never clarified.

A provisional balance sheet for Operation Turquoise shows that France must at least be credited with attempting something in the face of international indifference and with saving some thousands of Tutsi lives in the security zone, without the loss of a single French soldier. However, this can only be considered a relative success in comparison to the hundreds of thousands of victims of the genocide and the *a posteriori* realisation that if such a small action could be successful then it should have been possible to intervene over a far larger area.

The essentially negative factor in the intervention was France's determination to limit itself to an action that was strictly humanitarian, which their government regarded as the only way of ensuring that the security zone did not turn into the wasps' nest that it threatened to be. The French government did nothing that might have contributed to resolving the political problems of Rwanda. There was no attempt to curb or control the propaganda of the assassins who could both maintain and reinforce their control over the population in the 'secure humanitarian area'. And it certainly proved to be secure for the perpetrators of the genocide who could be sure that no action would be taken against them there. Radio Mille Collines continued to broadcast from the area until mid-July, without any attempt by the French military to find and destroy the transmitter.

As the last soldiers left Rwanda, France could not resist a display of self-congratulation. The chorus of praise, with hardly a single voice raised in protest, which accompanied the end of this operation is not fully justified: a major power such as France must achieve more in such a situation than can be accomplished by a humanitarian organisation. In Rwanda, the end of Operation Turquoise represented both France's disengagement from the search for a political solution, as well as what could perhaps be seen as the renewal of support to the ex-FAR government. France ensured that her former allies, the perpetrators of the genocide – and they were known to the government – were not arrested by French soldiers. Yet this was exactly what France *should* have done to demonstrate a desire for justice, to restore French credibility in regard to its history with Rwanda and so start working towards finding a political resolution to the conflict, beginning with the cutting of all links with the instigators of the genocide. When French troops finally left the security zone, the situation remained chaotic and led to further displacements within the zone and towards Zaire, the whole operation appearing to have done nothing more than to provide a temporary breathing space.

In summary, although Operation Turquoise helped to save several thousand Tutsi lives and to provide logistical help in Goma, it served principally as a public relations vehicle for France. France used the cover of a very limited but successful intervention to disguise the fact that, although it is one of the most powerful countries in the world, it was contributing nothing more than any other country towards finding a real political solution to this crisis.

The Limits of Humanitarian Action

By the end of June 1994, the crisis in Rwanda was seen exclusively as a humanitarian catastrophe affecting hundreds of thousands of refugees which aroused international compassion and distracted attention from the genocide that had more or less run its course at this point – for there were no more victims available for slaughter. The Tutsi that survived the slaughters had either fled the country or were internally displaced in areas already held by the RPF. No one knows exactly how many were killed, but it is certain that hundreds of thousands of Tutsi were 'eradicated'. With the RPF troops making rapid advances, the architects and instigators of the genocide then organised a mass exodus of the Hutu population. Broadcasting their propaganda over the radio, the successful campaign of intimidation forced the people to leave for Tanzania in May and June, then Goma (Zaire) and the French-controlled security zone in July. This was a deliberate strategy designed with a view to the future. The RPF advanced into a country that had been largely emptied of its people. As the security zone did not extend into north-west Rwanda, hundreds of thousands of people from this area fled into Goma and within a few days they had achieved the most rapid exodus of such large numbers of refugees in recorded history.

At that point news channels, such as CNN, and virtually every other television station in the world focused their cameras on this small country of the thousand hills and reported the story. Rwanda quickly found a place alongside Biafra, Ethiopia and Somalia in the list of humanitarian crises that have grabbed the world's attention. Contradicting pessimists who declared that the public was crisis-weary after Somalia and Bosnia and would not respond to yet another tragedy, an incredible surge of generosity swept across the world.

Goma was a hell on earth with cholera killing thousands of people every day. At the beginning of the epidemic, the daily mortality rate was 40 for every 10,000 people, which resulted in the loss of 50,000 people, or 5 per cent of the refugee population, in the first two weeks.

Even at this late stage in the crisis when the political problem of displaced people was obvious to all, the situation continued to be dealt with from an almost exclusively humanitarian angle. Would the refugees be able and willing to return to Rwanda? The UN seemed to follow no defined political line and inside Rwanda there was no international presence capable of reassuring those refugees who wanted to return home. At the beginning of August, the deployment of the UNAMIR II forces under the 17 May Security Council resolution was still being delayed. Kofi Anan, the Under Secretary-General in charge of the peacekeeping operation, gave reasons for the delays that read like a list of grievances. Caught between governments that offered troops and no equipment and other governments that offered the opposite, a lack of planes to transport men and equipment from the four corners of the earth, the UN's own financial crisis and its unwieldy administration, Kofi Anan and his team saw their margin for manoeuvre shrink. At the end of July, more than two months after the resolution had authorised the deployment of 5500 men, only 550 soldiers were in the field.

Other, more traditional problems, existed in the camps. Humanitarian aid, although well-intended and based on sound principles, can never be totally neutral for it represents almost the only source of food, equipment and jobs in the camps and thus becomes a major stake in the power struggle for control over the refugees. This is not, to the same extent, the case with medical assistance, which is easier to check up on. Food aid is much more difficult to control because of the vast quantities involved, making it almost impossible to keep responsibility for distribution from the hands of political groups who exert a powerful influence in the camps. Although there is a general impression that refugee camps comprise a mass of individual victims of a crisis, in reality there are always one or more political organisations at work struggling to gain control over them. Humanitarian workers are continually confronted with the same problem: how to aid the victims without becoming caught up in the power struggles of their oppressors, or, as William Shawcross puts it, how to feed the victims without also providing aid to their tormentors.[3] In this case it was the militias who were acting as the strong arm of the politicians in the camps.

In Benako, an isolated place that quickly became the second largest 'town' in Tanzania, nearly 300,000 refugees arrived within a few days with their leaders, the *bourgmestres*, the same men who had encouraged them to commit terrible crimes against the Tutsi. But a few dozen expatriates arriving in a country in a crisis situation cannot possibly be expected to cope with such an influx of refugees and resolve all the accompanying problems on their own without the assistance of local personnel. In the case of an emergency on this scale, the simplest answer is to use the existing infrastructure – in this case, the existing administrative system that was imported from Rwanda in the form of the *bourgmestres*. In Benako and Goma, the refugees organised themselves commune-by-commune under the direction of their local leaders. But the situation posed a major ethical problem: those in authority, criminals with a great deal of influence over the refugees, resisted any attempt at removal. In Rwanda, due to the large number of refugees, the polarisation of Rwandan society between Hutu and Tutsi and the exceptional character of the genocide, there was a particularly serious risk of the previous power structure consolidating and becoming capable of perpetuating an interminable conflict.

A parallel must be drawn here with Cambodia, where the Khmer Rouge were able to seize power through manipulating humanitarian aid. At the beginning of 1979, the Khmer Rouge, who were responsible for the massacre of a million of their fellow Cambodians, fled before the advancing Vietnamese army. Using force and propaganda, they took with them hundreds of thousands of civilians who then experienced a dreadful famine as refugees in the frontier area with Thailand. The international community mobilised, although more slowly than would happen today, and thousands of people were saved from a certain death. But the humanitarian effort also succeeded in feeding the Khmer Rouge and inadvertently helped them to establish their control over the refugee population. They were then able to establish a strong enough position to carry on the conflict for a further decade.[4]

Thus there are certainly similarities between the situations in Cambodia and the Rwandan refugee camps. The international humanitarian effort, which saved thousands of lives, risks sowing the seeds of a future conflict where the former government army, like the Khmer Rouge, will use their political control over hundreds of thousands of people in order to legitimise their power, their war and their revenge. But the international community seems totally blind to this very likely scenario. A vicious circle, fed by international aid, is gradually forming and, once again, it is made possible by treating the Rwandan crisis as a purely humanitarian matter when it is first and foremost a political issue. Several different measures were proposed to avoid the scenario becoming a reality (for example, deployment of human rights observers in Rwanda, increasing the amount of aid distributed directly through Kigali, and re-establishing the justice system as quickly as possible). If the right conditions had been facilitated, the humanitarian organisations are now convinced that most of the refugees would have returned home. As long as they are not, the world will have to assist two million refugees, possibly for several years; the war will very likely break out again and further aid will be required for future victims. As happened in Cambodia, this could turn into a long nightmare. Lack of political action thus risks a stronger negative effect on the situation than the positive effects of the solidarity that swept the world in 1994.

For Western governments, humanitarian action provided a way of responding to the crisis while continuing to conveniently overlook the fact that a genocide had taken place until the situation had evolved to such a point that it could be forgotten altogether. In a world where humanitarian aid seems almost the only form of international action in response to a crisis, aid that neither can nor will make a distinction between different categories of victim, all catastrophes are

treated alike and reduced to their lowest common denominator – the compassion of the observer. It is certainly the case
that each and every victim is equal and merits our care and
consideration, whether they be Tutsis suffering the result of
genocide, or their murderers stricken with cholera as refugees.
Humanitarian action is at the service of all victims: it seeks
to care for and feed them and does not take sides. But such
goodwill on its own is not enough, however, and humanitarian aid is useless if it is not accompanied by political
action and efforts to achieve justice. The Tutsi died out of
sight of the camera and with no help on hand. Governments
that practise humanitarianism are practising a policy that
claims nothing can be done in such a situation beyond caring
for the survivors. At the political and judiciary levels, the world
has no desire to act and the cameras are useless. In a recent
study, Nick Gowing of Britain's Channel Four television convincingly demonstrated from recent examples that television
pictures only have a short-term influence in launching
humanitarian operations and have almost no impact at all
on policy-making at the international level.[5]

Humanitarian action transforms any dramatic event –
crime, epidemic, natural disaster – into a catastrophe for
which, it seems, nobody is ever blamed. Humanitarianism
also masks the obligation and the necessity to intervene in
other ways. Often much too late, it is assumed that any
accusation of non-assistance can always be countered by
taking 'good' action. With the exception of some who may
speak out, how many would stand up in the midst of a catastrophe, when the donations are rolling in, to point out that,
in the wake of massacres, it is not enough to give food and
drink to people who have lost everything? Surely provision
of aid is merely the least that can be achieved. Unfortunately,
this kind of debate is only useful if it takes place during the
crisis. Afterwards, it is too late and eventually the mass
murders will be rehabilitated and become party to the debate.

It is no longer a question of struggling against the odds
to save lives. This is a crude way of describing a crisis
situation, which confuses everything, blurring essential distinctions and combining all the elements of a disaster so that
the overall problem is seen as a humanitarian one. It is no

longer even a question of criticising media operations such as the air evacuation of children, which is quite scandalous from an ethical perspective. Humanitarian action is itself in crisis, not for lack of the material means to accomplish its task, but rather for its inability to identify exactly what that task is.

In short, confronted in Rwanda with the first unquestionable genocide since that of the Jews, the world first reacted with indifference, leaving the country to its fate until the compassion aroused by the plight of the refugees led to a purely humanitarian intervention. This was a convenient way of distracting attention from the previous non-intervention at the political or military level and ensured that Western governments were seen as benign, now that they at least appeared to be doing something. By not taking a firm stand against the former criminal regime in Rwanda, the UN and the principal countries involved succeeded in remaining neutral in the face of the planned extermination of hundreds of thousands of people. But the concept of neutrality has no sense where a war of aggression or a genocide is concerned. As Chateaubriand, the French writer, put it: 'Such neutrality is derisory for it works against the weaker party and plays into the hands of the stronger party. It would be better to join forces with the oppressor against the oppressed for at least that would avoid adding hypocrisy to injustice.'

CHAPTER 5

Justice Must be Done

Taking humanitarian, rather than political, action is one of the best ways for a developed country to avoid facing up to its responsibilities in the wake of a disaster such as Rwanda. Another way is language. Employing a particular vocabulary can cast doubt on the actual causes of the massacre and foster confused images of the guilty and the victims. 'Warring parties', 'belligerents' and 'civil war' on one hand, and 'aggression', 'massacre' and 'genocide' on the other, are all strong words – but they are not synonymous in meaning. Under the cover of a supposed objectivity, to suggest that 'both parties' have committed atrocities can often be seen as an underhand way of giving them the same status. To speak of tribal disputes when an armed majority perpetrates a genocide against unarmed minority is patronising and meaningless. The aggression against the Bosnians and the genocide of the Tutsis both exceed civil war. In the case of Rwanda, to compare the RPF with the Rwandan Armed Forces (FAR) is at best a display of ignorance, at worst propaganda. The FAR have committed a genocide and the RPF have carried out exactions: the two things cannot be compared. If a distinction is not made, then genocide is reduced to the status of common murder – but murder is *not* the same as genocide. They differ both in nature and in degree, a fact that needs to be constantly emphasised if the crimes committed in Rwanda are not to be pushed to the back of international consciousness.

The perpetrators of genocide should permanently lose any legitimacy as rulers of their people. They should be outlawed by the international community and brought to trial for their crimes. In the case of Rwanda, no attempt should be made to negotiate with those responsible for the genocide

61

of the Tutsis: they are not only directly responsible for this worst possible crime against humanity but also for the exodus from Rwanda and the catastrophic events in Goma which followed. When the Allied forces won victory in 1945, there was never any question of providing a role for the Nazi party in the new Germany, nor of considering just how small a fraction of the population it really represented. The Nazis were banned outright and the authors of genocide then, as should happen in Rwanda today, lost any right to participate in public life.

Individual Guilt and Collective Responsibility

Karl Jaspers, the German philosopher, examined Germany's guilt in a book, published in 1990, that is still relevant today in the light of the recent events in Bosnia and Rwanda. He distinguished four types of culpability:

- *Criminal guilt*, of an individual in a case where the facts are not in doubt. The case will be dealt with by a court and punishment will be accorded. Such guilt is by definition individual. As Robert Jackson, the American prosecutor at Nuremberg, said, it 'makes no sense whatsoever to accuse a whole population of a crime'.
- *Political guilt* falls on every citizen of a guilty nation, even those who were opposed to the criminal acts involved. Here, sanctions are limited to reparations and restrictions on power and political rights.
- *Moral guilt* is shared by everyone who has not actively and sufficiently opposed the crime being committed. It represents the ultimate individual guilt, for only the individual conscience can be the judge of it.
- *Metaphysical guilt* results from the simple fact of living in a world where evil is everywhere.[1]

Finally, despite such distinctions, Karl Jaspers believes that there is an ultimate unity between these four categories of guilt in the form of a universal moral code which confers its authority onto the law when the law condemns the crime that only it can define.

The French political philosopher, Paul Ricoeur, commenting on Jaspers book, observes that the first and third types of guilt, which are individual, should be distinguished from the second and fourth types, which are collective. The word guilt actually only applies to the first and the third categories, both of which insinuate that an offence has been committed. Ricoeur disagrees with the concept of political guilt and instead favours a concept of political responsibility. This should result in sanctions aimed at the collective community, no matter the extent to which individual members participated in or resisted the criminal regime. Reparations, the loss of power and economic sanctions are collective sanctions which target individuals, inasmuch as they are citizens of a country. Such responsibility is collective, not individual, 'not because of the nature of the crime but because of the impossibility of dealing with the numbers involved'. The price of collective responsibility is itself collective in two ways, according to Ricoeur: sanctions which the individuals of the whole nation share to some extent through reparations; and culpability that brings together the collective sum total of individual offences. For Paul Ricoeur, the accusation of collective guilt is one caught between the twin dangers of the arbitrariness of the law and the moral hypocrisy of those who claim the right to sit in judgement.[2]

There is an urgent need for national reconciliation in Rwanda, but this must not be at the expense of justice, otherwise the opposite effect will be produced and the murderers reinstated. In Germany, at the end of the war, the Nazis and the democrats did not sit down together to discuss reconciliation. Likewise the international community should now give its support exclusively to the new, mainly RPF, government which is the legitimate government of Rwanda today. Its legitimacy does not come from the ballot box, but from its victory over a racist regime and its stated intention of working towards national reconciliation between the different groups and parties. But at the beginning of 1995, it seemed that the worst possible scenario was being realised with the FAR rallying huge number of refugees to take up the combat once again and 'finish off the job'. The slogan 'the Tutsis took 25 years to return with 200,000 refugees but we will only need a few weeks with two million to draw on' has been widely heard. Renewal of the conflict will simply lead the international community once again to justify its reasons for not getting involved: the (new) civil war, the RPF minority in the face of the 'reality of the Hutu majority'. And the genocide will be lost sight of, consigned to the history books.

Crime and Punishment

The lack of a global commitment for dealing with a crime of this scale represents not only a moral defeat on the part of the international community, but also a grave political error. Those who bear the greatest responsibility for the genocide must be brought to trial for three reasons.

First, of course, for the the the sake of the victims. The renaissance philosopher, Hugo Grotius, stated that punishment is necessary to defend the honour of the injured party who would otherwise be degraded if no punishment were accorded to his aggressor.

Second, if a killer is pursued under criminal law by a state because he has broken the laws of that state and community, not simply because he has deprived a family of one of its members, then the authors of a genocide should be pursued not only because they have killed hundreds of thousands of people, but, even more so, because they have violated the moral order of the human race by attempting to destroy one of its member parts. There is no future for humanity if one, cohesive, part of it risks extermination by another whose members will never be punished. Lemkin first made the point that Hannah Arendt later expanded upon:

> The extermination of entire ethnic groups, Jews, Poles or the Gypsy people, might be more than a crime against the Jewish or the Polish people and the Gypsy people ... the international order and mankind in its entirety might have been grievously hurt and endangered.[3]

Arendt added, 'If genocide is an actual possibility of the future, then no people on earth ... can feel reasonably sure of its continued existence without the help and protection of international laws.'[4] This is the reasoning behind the statement made to the judges at the Nuremberg Trials by Robert Jackson, that the real plaintiff before the court was Civilization itself. That is also precisely why the Convention on the Prevention and Punishment of the Crime of Genocide commits its signatories 'to punish and prevent genocide' and why it covers 'genocide, conspiracy to commit genocide, direct and public incitement to commit genocide, attempt to commit genocide and complicity in genocide'.*

The third and final reason is the political imperative that those responsible for the genocide in Rwanda should be punished. If this does not happen, the whole world, but particularly Africa, risks being caught up in a spiral of violence and there is enormous potential for further ethnic cleansing and genocide. Only the assurance of world order can ensure that genocide is not repeated. World order in the post-Second World War period has been built on the basis of that famous slogan 'Never again!'. And yet, not only are we once again seeing war waged in Europe, the world has also witnessed the first real genocide in 50 years. If the response of the international community is only in the form of humanitarian action, with no regard for ensuring that justice is done, this surely will result in a frightening regression in our moral order and will, in effect, give the go-ahead to any would-be dictators tempted to manipulate 'the ethnic question' to resolve, or distract from, their own political problems.

Trials must be held, not only for the victims themselves, but even more so for the moral order throughout international society, which is under grave threat if further abominations of a similar kind are encouraged through a lack of resolve and political will.

Four categories of responsibility can be identified:

1. Those who instigate the plot. Genocide does not happen by chance nor out of spontaneous collective madness and in Rwanda, the plan was conceived by a small core of people close to President Habyarimana. It was they

---

* See Appendix 1.

who drew up the blueprints for the militias, death squads and Radio Mille Collines, even if they were not the ones to transform them into a reality: they made sure that there was no blood on their hands. Nevertheless, there is no question that these are the most guilty and must be made to stand trial before an international tribunal.

2. The levels of administrative hierarchy in Rwanda (the *bourgmestres* or mayors, the armed forces, the militia heads, etc.). These, too, would claim to have 'clean hands' – as did Eichmann – and may well try to plead like the Nazis that they were only obeying orders, and had no choice: that they were only the cogs in a large machine. They will no doubt claim that 'everybody else' participated in the genocide and so they should not stand trial unless 'everybody else' stands alongside them. Let Hannah Arendt's words on the Eichmann verdict answer them:

> Guilt and innocence before the law are of an objective nature, and even if 80 million Germans had done as you did, this would not have been an excuse for you ... We are concerned here only with what you did ... Let us assume, for the sake of argument, that it was nothing more than misfortune that made you a willing instrument in the organisation of mass murder; there still remains the fact that you have carried out, and therefore actively supported, a policy of mass murder. For politics is not like the nursery; in politics obedience and support are the same. And just as you supported and carried out a policy of not wanting to share the earth with the Jewish people ... as though you and your superiors had any right to determine who should and who should not inhabit the world – we find that no one, that is, no member of the human race, can be expected to want to share the earth with you. This is the reason, and the only reason, you must hang.[5]

3. Those who profited from the situation and the general climate of violence, and apparent impunity, to carry out

particularly sadistic and odious acts. Whenever they can be identified, they should be brought to trial.

4. Finally, there are the thousands of people who represent the majority of the guilty but who killed out of fear, because they were ordered to do so or because they were caught up in that situation of collective murder created by the authorities and the militias. Everybody had to take part: carrying a stick to break a Tutsi skull was a way of proving 'non-allegiance to the RPF'. Refusal to kill was likely to lead directly to being killed. But a crime remains a crime, even when it is committed under duress and every murderer should, in principle, have to face some kind of trial.

The fourth category, however, does present a problem: the numbers involved – tens of thousands of individuals – is so great that it would be administratively impossible to judge all of them. It is better to admit this from the start to avoid it being used as a major argument against actioning the first two categories. Although there were many Germans who were interned in concentration camps as early as 1933 because of their opposition to the rise of national socialism, the scale of that genocide would have been impossible if the Nazis had not been able to depend on the German people as a whole through the organised bureaucracy of the state, what Hannah Arendt describes as 'the rule of Nobody'. But this argument was never used to prevent the trials going ahead. The massacres of Jews, just like those of Tutsis, were committed anonymously and it would be very difficult, although there are exceptional cases, to attribute the murder to any one Tutsi or to any one Hutu in particular. But this anonymity also masks the seriousness of the crime, to avoid the questions concerning guilt and responsibility: in short, it enables behaviour as though nothing has happened.[6] Not all the guilty were judged in Germany, but the most important thing is that some were: at least some of those responsible paid for their crime. The Nazi ideology was outlawed and those who supported it openly were forced out of official posts and excluded from political life in general.

The Hutu accused in any eventual trial are bound to plead extenuating circumstances, inflated statistics, the prevailing climate of war and the illegitimacy of a justice system operated by their recent adversaries. None of these are valid arguments.

The question of statistics, in particular, is wholly irrelevant. Nobody knows exactly how many Tutsis died and under such circumstances, anybody producing figures would very likely be tempted to inflate them. Certainly there were not as many as a million deaths, a figure which has sometimes been put forward. Half a million is a more than safe estimate. If the population of Rwanda is estimated at 7 million, with Tutsis making up 15 per cent of that number, the figure of 500,000 deaths would represent half of the Tutsis living in the interior of the country. It is possible that the final toll will be even higher. But although we will never know exactly how many died, this should not be used to lessen the significance of the crime itself. It is not necessary to speculate on the exact final figure for the number of deaths. There was a genocide last year in Rwanda. That is a fact, not speculation.

That the country was at war following the new RPF offensive after the death of the president and the fact that the RPF was suported by many Tutsis, do not represent 'extenuating circumstances' for they can neither explain nor justify the attempted killing of the whole Tutsi people. Genocide has nothing to do with war. In the examples of both Germany and Rwanda, war is a context in which genocide can take place.

As to whether or not the winning party can legitimately constitute a tribunal, Karl Jaspers considered that the most important issue for Germans at the end of the Second World War was that 'we did not free ourselves from the criminal regime, but rather were freed from it by the allied forces'.[7] If the victors can raise their victory to a legal status, it gives meaning to the violence that has taken place. Jaspers believed that the powerless losers do not ask the victors to forgive them, but to give a meaning to the sentence that is pronounced. Thus, if Israel and France had the right to judge Eichmann and Barbie, then the RPF-backed Rwandan government has the right to judge the perpetrators of the genocide.

But justice in Rwanda will be no easy matter. The legal system under the previous regime was already seriously deficient in many areas, suffering from a lack of judges, poor training, political meddling and nepotism. Today there are even fewer judges and magistrates. They, along with the main people involved in the movement for democracy under Habyarimana, were high on the lists of those to be eliminated by the Hutu militia. Even supposing that its intentions are sincere, the new government will have to face enormous practical difficulties in organising fair trials. This is why the people mainly responsible for the plot should stand before an international tribunal. Others may be tried in Rwanda itself but, even so, the country will require assistance from the United Nations, other countries and non-governmental organisations in order to do this. Rwanda is just beginning to come out of deep trauma and already the new government is assailed by critics who invoke one-sided human rights arguments – although their voices were strangely silent through the years before the killings. The Tutsi people alive today have survived weeks of genocidal slaughter. This is not the time to focus solely on issues of human rights. They need a helping hand in the gigantic task of reconstruction and reconciliation that lies ahead, not accusations of a deliberate policy of revenge.

By an extraordinary and yet inevitable paradox, the world had no precise details of the massacres during the genocide, but as soon as the country was once more accessible to the media, the most minor human rights violation was reported and judged by the press and foreign observers. So some caution is needed before making a blanket condemnation of the new regime on the basis of individual acts. A discerning commentator would not confuse a systematic policy with an isolated event and it is essential that we do not lose sight of the fact that more than five per cent of the population was killed in a matter of eight weeks and that five per cent constitutes the larger part of the minority group. We must also keep in mind that the wholesale slaughter comprised hundreds of thousands of individual acts. It is worth remembering that, throughout the Second World War, France lost two per cent of the civilian population and Germany six per cent. We should also recall the reprisals that followed the liberation of France.

The racist philosophy of the previous Hutu government and the dangers of trivialising, and even forgetting, the events of last summer are summed up perfectly in a remarkable interview with François Karera, the former mayor of Kigali, now living comfortably with his family in Zaire, just a few miles from the misery of the refugee camps (one of which he is responsible for). According to Karera 'The Tutsis are originally bad. They are murderers. The Tutsis have given the white people their daughters. Physically they are weak – look at their arms and legs. No Tutsi can build: they are too weak ... they just command ... The others work.'[8] The Hutus were determined, Karera said, not to allow the Tutsis to repeat history and to slay the Hutus as they did 400 years ago. 'If the reasons are just, the massacres are justified. In war you don't consider the consequences, you consider the causes. ... We cannot use that word genocide because there are numerous survivors.'[9] He anticipates a future (Hutu) government that would also contain Tutsi representatives, but on a proportional basis to their numbers in the population because, he says, 'that's democracy'.

Karera would presumably reject political scientist Lijphart's theory that in a society composed of different ethnic groups, when power lies in the hands of the one which represents the significant majority, the ground is far better prepared for dictatorship and civil war than for democracy. Thus, what this kind of society requires, is a democratic regime which stresses consensus rather than opposition, which is inclusive rather than exclusive, and which tries to maximise support for itself rather than being satisfied with a simple majority: in other words, 'a democracy of consensus'.[10]

It is François Karera, and his like, who prevent the refugees from returning home. His 'reasoning' has nothing to do with majorities: it is based on racism. There is a great fear that people like him may be reinstated by the international community through the politics of humanitarian aid and the misconceived belief that the right to rule automatically belongs exclusively to the majority group.

Political Responsibility: Belgium, France and the United States

Belgium, France and the United States must accept a degree of responsibility for this genocide. Belgium is responsible for having largely created the political antagonism between the Hutus and Tutsis and then transforming it into a racial problem which sowed the seeds of the present tragedy. France closed its eyes to the growing racism at the heart of the system and the increasing number of massacres over the past four years and continued to support the former regime to the bitter end. The subsequent actions of the French government to protect the Tutsis cannot balance out the weight of the past. The United States can be accused of not taking up its moral responsibility as the major world power, blocking the initiatives of UN Secretary-General Boutros Boutros-Ghali and preventing US officials from using the word genocide to sidestep the international obligation to intervene that recognition of the crime would have imposed. President Clinton, finally moved to intervene after the screening of CNN film of the camps in Goma, limited United States involvement only to humanitarian assistance. The only really positive note was the surprising (given their experience over Somalia) degree of support from the American people.

However, the very positive degree of humanitarian support given by many countries cannot absolve them of an abdication of responsible action. It is now up to the United States, Belgium, France and the other countries of the European Union to work towards bringing the criminals to trial and helping in the reconstruction of Rwanda. These are political responsibilities that must be acknowledged and accepted by countries, either in the light of their past role in Rwanda, or of their present world status.

A New Militancy?

If war should break out again in Rwanda, there will be a strong temptation on the part of Western countries to forget the recent past in the name of reconciliation, fatalism, tribalism, amnesia or amnesty. This must be resisted as it would represent a form of racism and rejection of Africa that goes against all we claim to believe in. Even if neither the nature nor the degree of the crimes committed by the Hutus are comparable to the factory death camps of the Nazis, they are both genocides. It is therefore to the Nuremberg Trials that we must turn for the only example we have of how to proceed in pursuing those responsible for the genocide. As the only precedent we have, it must neither be ignored nor rejected as irrelevant.

The *ad hoc* International Tribunal set up in The Hague to deal with the crimes committed in the former Yugoslavia will be a first test of international determination to deal with such matters in the 1990s. Even if it is not perfect and even if the proceedings are very long drawn-out – the Nuremberg Trials started five months after the end of hostilities and lasted for a year – this court could provide a precedent for other crimes against humanity committed in other parts of the world. A second test will be the International Tribunal for Rwanda which has been set up in Arusha, Tanzania, and will deal with the principal people behind the genocide. The culprits will not be hard to find: names are known and many are even walking around freely in Paris, Brussels and Montreal. However, it is far from certain that the Tribunal will receive the necessary financial support and backing from UN member states to do a convincing job.

Therefore, it would be a mistake for human rights militants to place too much faith in international bodies. The international community has a tendency to show great enthusiasm for setting up new institutions and introducing legislation that, ultimately, serves only to hide its inability to actually do anything. For example, the nomination of a High Commissioner for Human Rights is barely a step forward considering the restricted mandate that has been given. It could become an effective role if Ayala Lasso, the first person appointed to the post, takes a sufficiently public stand on human rights abuses in much the same way as Sadoko Ogata, the current UN High Commissioner for Refugees, has in regard to refugees.

Concerned individuals need to use more efficient tactics to put pressure on their governments to act. The Rwanda crisis not only sheds more light on the failure of the UN and its principal member governments, it also reflects on the neutrality stand taken by humanitarian organisations and on human rights organisations. Whereas the latter once effectively breached the defences around national sovereignty during the Cold War era when this was zealously protected by individual states, they seem to have little impact on civil wars, crimes against humanity or incidents of blatant aggression. There seems little to be gained by adding reports from Amnesty International to those already written by Tadeusz Mazowiecki or René Degni-Ségui, the official UN rapporteurs for Bosnia and Rwanda respectively. Such isolated indignation, report writing and press releases no longer work, although, personally, I have the greatest respect for the commitment of those who work for such organisations. Certainly, such methods are still useful in acting against validly constituted governments that violate the human rights of their citizens; and countless thousands of political prisoners owe their lives to them. But many such organisations continue to operate as if the world has not changed in the past few years. There are other methods that could be used today, particularly action in the field. It is not a question of taking over the role of the state, but rather of forcing action upon them. Rather than calling on the UN to deploy human rights observers in Rwanda or in other countries, why do human rights organisations not do the job themselves? Rather than wait for some hypothetical international justice to arrive, why do they not carry out 'trial by media' of these war criminals? Why not, wherever possible, use the existing legal systems of those countries that allow action to be taken on war crimes and crimes against humanity committed elsewhere? The opening up of countries since the end of the Cold War has created a new situation that requires alternative strategies from human rights organisations.

Human life is so much more than mere biology and human need cannot be fully met by humanitarian action alone, although this is, generally, the only response to world tragedies. This is not to deny the importance of such action, but it should only be employed in tandem with other forms of intervention. The purpose is not so much to save lives; it is to save human beings, something quite different. Where justice and reason are lacking, the human solidarity that replaces them, such as was displayed at Goma – but too late to save the victims of the genocide – is worth nothing. It is the moral responsibility of each one of us, citizens of this planet, to contribute something to prevent this unique event from being forgotten, even before it has been properly recognised.

Convention on the Prevention and Punishment of the Crime of Genocide

Approved by the General Assembly of the United Nations in Resolution 260 A (III) of 9 December 1948. Came into effect on 12 January 1951.

The Contracting Parties,

Having considered the declaration made by the General Assembly of the United Nations in its resolution 96 (I) dated 11 December 1946 that genocide is a crime under international law, contrary to the spirit and aims of the United Nations and condemned by the civilised world;

Recognising that at all periods of history genocide has inflicted great losses on humanity;

and

Being convinced that, in order to liberate mankind from such an odious scourge, international cooperation is required,

Hereby agrees as hereinafter provided:

Article I

The Contracting Parties confirm that genocide, whether committed in time of peace or in time of war, is a crime under international law which they undertake to prevent and to punish.

Article II

In the present Convention, genocide means any of the following acts committed with intent to destroy, in whole or in part, a national, ethnical, racial or religious group, as such:

a Killing members of the group;
b Causing serious bodily or mental harm to members of the group;
c Deliberately inflicting on the group conditions of life calculated to bring about its physical destruction in whole or in part;
d Imposing measures intended to prevent births within the group;
e Forcibly transferring children of the group to another group.

Article III

The following acts shall be punishable:

a Genocide;
b Conspiracy to commit genocide;
c Direct and public incitement to commit genocide;
d Attempt to commit genocide;
e Complicity in genocide.

Article IV

Persons committing genocide or any of the other acts enumerated in Article III shall be punished, whether they are constitutionally responsible rulers, public officials or private individuals.

Article V

The Contracting Parties undertake to enact, in accordance with their respective Constitutions, the necessary legislation to give effect to the provisions of the present Convention and, in particular, to provide effective penalties for persons guilty of genocide or of any of the other acts enumerated in Article III.

Article VI

Persons charged with genocide or any of the other acts enumerated in Article III shall be tried by a competent tribunal of the State in the territory of which the act was committed, or by such international penal tribunal as may have jurisdiction with respect to those Contracting Parties which shall have accepted its jurisdiction.

Article VII

Genocide and the other acts enumerated in Article III shall not be considered as political crimes for the purpose of extradition.
The Contracting Parties pledge themselves in such cases to grant extradition in accordance with their laws and treaties in force.

Article VIII

Any Contracting Party may call upon the competent organs of the United Nations to take such action under the Charter of the United Nations as they consider appropriate for the prevention and suppression of acts of genocide or any of the other acts enumerated in Article III.

Article IX

Disputes between the Contracting Parties relating to the interpretation, application or fulfilment of the present Convention, including those relating to the responsibility of a State for genocide or for any other acts enumerated in Article III, shall be submitted to the International Court of Justice at the request of any of the parties to the dispute.

(Articles X to XIX are concerned with technicalities.)

Note: The Convention has been ratified by more than 120 States. Rwanda acceded in 1975. The Convention is considered to be part of generally accepted international law. The International Court of Justice confirmed this in 1951.

Rwanda: A Chronology

1885	The Berlin Conference decides that the region should become the responsibility of the German Empire.
1908	A German military command is installed in Kigali but power continues to be exercised though the Mwami, the head of a Tutsi dynasty.
After the First World War 1924	Belgium accepts the mandate of the League of Nations to administer Rwanda and Burundi.
1931	Mwami Musinga is deposed by the Belgians.
After the Second World War	The UN confers the mandate for Rwanda and Burundi onto Belgium with a commitment to 'emancipation'.
1957	Publication of the Hutu Manifesto calling for Hutu independence from the Belgians and the Tutsi monarchy.
1959	A bloody Hutu revolt leads to Rwanda being placed under military government. The massacre of 20,000 Tutsi results in a first exodus, mainly to Uganda.
1961	The Parmehutu (party of the Hutu) seizes power, abolishes the monarchy and proclaims a republic. This is confirmed by a majority of 80 per cent in a referendum a few months later.
1962	Independence is declared. Election of a Hutu president, Grégoire Kayibanda, who nominates only Hutus to his government.

1963 and 1967	Unsuccessful attempts by Tutsis of the diaspora to return by force on two occasions result in anti-Tutsi pogroms.
1973	President Kayibanda is overthrown in a bloodless coup d'état by the head of the armed forces, Juvénal Habyarimana, who imposes a 10 per cent quota on Tutsis employed in civil service and teaching posts. He refuses to deal with the question of the return of the Tutsi exiles.
1988	Creation of the Rwandan Patriotic Front (RPF) in Uganda grouping together exiled Tutsis and dissident Hutus.
1989	Setting up of a special commission dealing with the problems of Rwandan emigrants.
1990	
5 July	President Habyarimana announces the creation of a national commission to draw up a political charter.
1 October	The RPF launches an attack on the northeast of the country from Uganda. This leads to the arrest of thousands of Tutsis, accused of being RPF 'accomplices'.
4 October	Belgium and France send in troops to protect and evacuate their nationals.
8 October	The Rwandan army massacres between 500 and 1000 Hima du Mutura (a Tutsi subgroup).
11–13 October	Massacres of around 400 Tutsi in the commune of Kibilira.
End October	The RPF is pushed back into Uganda. Start of a guerrilla war. Belgium withdraws troops but a French contingent remains stationed in Rwanda.
13 November	President Habyarimana announces that other political parties will be allowed to form and the suppression of any mention of ethnic group on identity cards. The latter measure is never carried out.

1991

End January– Mid-March	Massacre of 500 to 1000 Bagogwe (a Tutsi sub-group) in the northwest of the country.
End March	Publication of the draft of the national charter and proposals for a constitution and a law in regard to political parties.
10 June	Promulgation of a new constitution recognising Rwanda as a multi-party state.
July	Assent is given to the creation of the first opposition parties: social-democrats, liberals and Christian-democrats.

1992

Beginning March	Massacres in the Bugesera region with at least 300 deaths.
May	RPF offensive takes over some communes in the extreme north of Rwanda and leads to the displacement of around 350,000 people.
12 July	Ceasefire is signed between the RPF and the Rwandan government.

1993

7–21 January	Visit by an international team investigating human rights violations in Rwanda since 1 October 1990.
8 February	RPF offensive in the north of the country which provokes the exodus of a million Hutus. The RPF carries out summary executions and France responds by sending an additional attachment of 300 men complete with heavy armour.
7 March	Ceasefire signed in Dar-es-Salaam.
8 March	The international investigation team publishes report condemning human rights violations in Rwanda. Belgium recalls her ambassador and other European countries threaten sanctions.
7 April	The Rwandan government acknowledges the report but denies both the existence of 'death squads' and that some of these incidents were planned in advance.

9 June	A protocol is signed in Arusha, Tanzania, in regard to the repatriation of refugees and the reinstallation of displaced people.
4 August	Peace accords signed in Arusha between the government and the RPF. They anticipate the installation of a transition government to include the RPF, fusion of the two armies, the deployment of the UN Assistance Mission for Rwanda (UNAMIR) and the demilitarisation of Kigali.
5 October	UN Security Council Resolution 872 authorises the creation of UNAMIR with 2500 soldiers and military observers to be provided from among 23 countries.
1 November	UNAMIR starts to deploy.
28 December	The RPF arrives in Kigali.
1994	
5 April	Security Council Resolution 909 extends the UNAMIR mandate till 29 July.
6 April	President Habyarimana and his colleague, President Cyprien Ntariyamira of Burundi are killed in a plane crash. The killings start in Kigali.
9 April	Belgian and French paratroopers arrive in Kigali to evacuate expatriates.
12 April	Beginning of the battle for Kigali between the government forces and the RPF. Tutsis are victims of massacres throughout the country.
21 April	Security Council Resolution 912 reduces the number of Blue Helmets in Rwanda to 270 and redefines the mandate of the UNAMIR force.
17 May	Security Council Resolution 918 calls for an end to hostilities, a ceasefire and the end of the massacres. The UNAMIR mandate is extended in order to protect people and areas under threat and increases the force to a maximum of 5500 (UNAMIR II).

25 May	The Human Rights Commission unanimously adopts a softly-worded resolution which states that acts of genocide may have been committed and authorises a Special Rapporteur to carry out an inquiry.
8 June	Security Council Resolution 925 extends the UNAMIR mandate until 9 December.
10 June	The Archbishop of Kigali, two bishops and ten priests are killed by RPF soldiers while under their protection.
11 June	The Ministerial Council of the Organisation of African States adopts a resolution calling for a ceasefire in Rwanda, condemning the massacres and describing them as a crime against humanity. France announces that she is prepared to intervene together with her European partners.
17 June	Boutros Boutros-Ghali gives his support to the French initiative for a humanitarian intervention.
22 June	Security Council Resolution 929 authorises France and other countries that might take part in the humanitarian operation to employ all necessary means during a two-month period to protect civilians and ensure the distribution of food aid.
30 June	The UN Human Rights Commission Special Rapporteur presents his report which describes the massacres as 'genocide'. The killings of moderate Hutus are qualified as political assassinations. He recommends either the creation of an international court to try those reponsible for the crimes committed in Rwanda or an extension to the mandate for the international tribunal dealing with crimes committed in former-Yugoslavia.
1 July	Security Council Resolution 935 calls for the formation of an impartial committee of experts to investigate the evidence for 'possible acts of genocide'.

3 July	There is a confrontation involving members of the RPF and French soldiers attached to Operation Turquoise.
4 July	RPF forces succeed in capturing Kigali.
5 July	France sets up 'a secure humanitarian area' in the south-west of Rwanda.
14 July	The RPF takes Ruhengeri, the main town in the north of the country, triggering a massive exodus of Rwandans towards Goma, Zaire.
17 July	Gisenyi, the last bastion of the government forces, falls to the RPF.
18 July	The RPF declares the end of the war and installs a new government with Pasteur Bizimungu as president, and Faustin Twagiramungu as prime minister, both Hutu. A body of 80 representatives, chosen by consensus between all the parties, with the exception of the extremist Hutu parties, is to be convoked in August.
21 July	Cholera is confirmed among the refugees in Goma.
22 July	President Clinton announces an American aid plan. Immense degree of solidarity is demonstrated throughout the world.
26 July	Start-up of 'Operation Hope' by the US.
29 July	France announces the beginning of troop withdrawals.
31 July	The US deploys a first contingent of soldiers in Kigali.
21 August	Departure of the last French troops from the security zone. Significant population movements within the zone towards Bukavu, Zaire.
End August	The security situation within the camps in Zaire deteriorates badly due to the activities of ex-government army troops .

Notes

Chapter 1: The Unlearned Lesson of History

1 Primo Levi, *Se questo è un vomo* (Turin: Guilo Einudi, 1958).
2 Raphaël Lemkin, *Axis Rule in Occupied Europe* (Washington: Carnegie Endowment for International Peace, 1944).
3 André Frossard, *Le crime contre l'humanité* (Paris: Robert Laffont, 1987).
4 Ibid.
5 Vladimir Jankélévitch, *L'imprescriptible* (Paris: Seuil, 1986).
6 Alain Finkielkraut, *La mémoire vaine. Du Crime contre l'humanité* (Paris: Gallimard, NRF essais, 1989).
7 Lemkin, *Axis Rule in Occupied Europe.*
8 Joe Verhoeven, *Le crime de génocide. Originalité et ambiguïté, Revue belge de droit international* (Brussels: éditions Bruylant, 1991).
9 Finkielkraut, *La mémoire vaine.*
10 Robert Conquest, *Harvest of Sorrows* (Oxford: Oxford University Press, 1987).
11 Guy Richard, *L'histoire inhumaine: massacres et génocides des origines à nos jours* (Paris: Armand Colin, 1992).
12 Georges de Maleville, *La tragédie arménienne de 1915* (Paris: éditions Lanore, 1988).
13 Ibid.
14 Quoted in Jankélévitch, *L'imprescriptible.*
15 Lemkin, *Axis Rule in Occupied Europe.*
16 J. Verhoeven, *Le crime de génocide.*

17 Alain Destexhe, 'Why Famine?', in François Jean and Anne-Marie Huby (eds), *Populations in Danger* (London: John Libbe/Médecins Sans Frontières, 1992).

18 Stephen Smith, *Somalie: La guerre perdue de l'humanitaire* (Paris: Calmann Lévy, 1993).

19 François Jean, *Du bon usage de la famine* (Paris: Médecins Sans Frontières, 1986).

20 John de Saint Jorre, *The Nigerian Civil War* (London: Hodder and Stoughton, 1972).

21 Quoted in Alfred Grosser, *Le crime et la mémoire* (Paris: Flammarion, 1989).

22 Lemkin, *Axis Rule in Occupied Europe.*

23 Raul Hilberg, *The Destruction of European Jews* (Quadrangle Books, 19661).

Chapter 2: Three Genocides in the Twentieth Century

1 Quoted in the foreword to the French version of Johannes Lepsius's secret report.

2 It is impossible to give precise figures as there was no census on which they can be based.

3 Bernard Lewis in *le Monde*.

4 Gérard Chaliand and Yves Ternon, *Le génocide des Arméniens* (Brussels: éditions Complexe, 1991).

5 Hannah Arendt, *Eichmann in Jerusalem* (Harmondsworth: Penguin, 1994).

6 In Burundi, massacres of Hutus and Tutsis took place in 1972, 1988 and 1993. In Rwanda, massacres of Tutsis took place in 1959–63, 1973 and since 1990.

7 FAR document, September 1992.

8 Jean-Pierre Chrétien, 'Un nazisme tropical', *Libération*, 26 April 1994; '"Just Like the Nazis", says Rwandan Rancher', the *Guardian*, 2 May 1994. Although comparison with Nazism is inadequate, there is no other precedent with which to compare what happened. See also Hooly Burckhalter, 'Make the Rwandan Killers' Bosses Halt this Genocide', *International Herald Tribune*, 2 May 1994, and Alison Desforges, 'How Governments Can Stop the Genocide in Rwanda', *New York Times*,

11 May 1994. Alain Juppé, the French Foreign Minister, used the word reservedly for the first time on 16 May 1994.

9   Quoted in Hilberg, *The Destruction of the European Jews*.
10   Although many Germans were indifferent to the deportation of Jews, many others did what they could to save individual Jews. The authorities were swamped by requests for exemptions from the friends, colleagues and acquaintances of Jews issued with deportation orders.
11   Quoted in Hilberg, *The Destruction of the European Jews*.

Chapter 3: *The Hutu and the Tutsi*

1   The 'ethnists', represented by Filip Reyntjens and Réné Lemarchand, are sometimes seen in opposition to the 'anti-ethnists', represented by Jean-Pierre Chrétien and Claudine Vidal. Unfortunately the works of these experts on Central Africa have not been translated into English.
2   Jean-Pierre Chrétien, *Burundi, l'histoire retrouvée* (Paris: Karthala, 1993).
3   Ibid.
4   This hypothesis originated with the British explorer J.H. Speke in 1863 and references to it continue as late as 1945.
5   Joseph Arthur Gobineau, *Essai sur l'inégalité des races humaines* (Paris: 1855).
6   Jean-Pierre Chrétien, 'Hutu et Tutsi au Rwanda et au Burundi', in Jean-Loup Amselle and Elikie M'Bokolo (eds), *Au coeur de l'ethnie. Ethnies, tribalisme et Etat en Afrique* (Paris: La Découverte, 1985), and Filip Reyntjens, *L'Afrique des grands lacs en crise. Rwanda, Burundi: 1988–1994* (Paris: Karthala, 1994).
7   J. Sasserath, *Le Ruanda-Urundi, étrange royaume féodal* (Brussels: 1948).
8   Ibid.
9   Louis De Lacger, *Ruanda* (Rwanda: Kabgayi, second edition 1961).
10   Omer Marchal, *Pleure, ô Rwanda bien-aimé* (Vaillance-en-Ardenne: Omer Marchal Editeur 1994).

11 Bahutu Manifesto: A note on the social aspects of the indigenous racial problem in Rwanda, 1957 unpublished paper.
12 Michel Elias and Danielle Helbig, 'Deux mille collines pour les petits et les grands', *Politique africaine*, No. 42, June 1991.
13 Claudine Vidal, *Sociologie des passions* (Paris: Karthala, 1991).
14. A detailed history of the RPF lies outside the scope of this book. See Gérard Prunier, 'Elément pour une histoire du Front patriotique Rwandais', *Politique africaine*, No. 51, October 1993. This article challenges a number of stereotypes connected with the RPF, particularly regarding its ethnic composition.
15 Elias and Helbig, 'Deux mille Collines'.

Chapter 4: From Indifference to Compassion

1 *Presidential Decision Directive: The Clinton Administration's Policy on Reforming Multilateral Peace Operations* (Washington: Department of State Publication 10161, May 1994).
2 *Independent*, 18 May 1994.
3 See Jean-Christophe Rufin, *Le piège humanitaire* (Paris: Jean-Claude Lattès, 1986) and William Shawcross, *The Quality of Mercy: Cambodia, Holocaust and Modern Conscience* (New York: Simon and Schuster, 1984).
4 Alain Destexhe, *L'humanitaire impossible ou deux siècles d'ambiguités* (Paris: Armand Colin, 1993); and Shawcross, *The Quality of Mercy*.
5 Nick Gowing, *Real-time Television Coverage of Armed Conflicts and Diplomatic Crises: Does it Pressure or Distort Foreign Policy Decision?* (Cambridge, MA: The Joan Shorenstein Barone Center, John F. Kennedy School of Government, Harvard University, 1994), and 'Images That Cry Out For Action', *International Herald Tribune*, 2 August 1994.

Chapter 5: *Justice Must be Done*

1 Karl Jaspers, *La culpabilité allemande* (Paris: Les Editions de Minuit, 1990).
2 Paul Ricoeur, *Lectures 1. Autour du politique* (Paris: Seuil, 1991).
3 Lemkin, *Axis Rule in Occupied Europe.*
4 Arendt, *Eichmann in Jerusalem.*
5 Ibid.
6 Pierre Vidal-Naquet, *Les Juifs, la mémoire et le présent* (Paris: La Découverte, 1991).
7 Jaspers, *La culpabilité allemande.*
8 *International Herald Tribune*, 16 August 1994.
9 Ibid.
10 Quoted in Filip Reyntjens, *L'Afrique des grands lacs en crise.*

Index